Compensating
Key Executives
in the Smaller Company

Compensating
Key Executives
in the Smaller Company

Theodore Cohn
Roy A. Lindberg

A Division of American Management Associations

Library of Congress Cataloging in Publication Data

Cohn, Theodore.
    Compensating key executives in the smaller company.

    Includes index.
    1. Executives—Salaries, pensions, etc.—United
States. 2. Compensation management—United States.
3. Small business—United States—Personnel management.
I. Lindberg, Roy A., joint author. II. Title.
HD4965.5.U6C63   658.4'07'220973   79-21221
ISBN 0-8144-5573-5

First Printing

Preface

THIS is a book on how to use compensation as a productive force in smaller companies. As we, the authors, see it, justification for the book exists in the facts that small companies cannot operate as do large companies, that an imaginative and up-to-date book on small-company compensation does not now exist, and that most books on compensation are, like financial statements, oriented to the past.

Moreover, we also want to put forth a few, possibly new ideas on the subject. For example, nowhere in the literature that we know of are motivation, IRS acceptable deductions (nontaxable to recipients), performance measurement, and individualized contribution in the smaller company dealt with in combination or on a trade-off basis.

Most managers we know think of compensation as a rather unpleasant problem, as something that has to be given, rather than as a *resource,* an element of the business to be managed toward selected objectives. Like any other resource, such as working capital or production materials, compensation offers any firm many opportunities to realize its aims more efficiently. We hope the book will convey that message convincingly.

For the most part, the book is addressed to the questions involved in paying *key* executives, that is, executives whose performance has a critical impact on their firms. Paying other employees is not less consequential in smaller than in larger firms, but the problems involved in paying them are not really size-related. The determinants and the constraints which dictate the amounts and terms of pay at lower levels or to more routinely performing executives are pretty much the same in all companies.

In smaller companies, however, the compensation of key executives is not as sensitive to conventions and common influences; it responds to so many variables that it easily falls victim to prejudices and false assumptions. Few business problems in smaller companies are more difficult to solve or have more impact in their solutions than deciding how best to pay key executives.

The connections between compensation, loyalty, productivity, and the other variables affecting and affected by pay escape most small-company managers. They tend to deal with these connections on an ad hoc basis, without objective knowledge or measures of performance. True, neither the fixing of pay nor the measuring of performance will ever be scientific. Nevertheless, much is known relevant to compensation that is factually based. Since compensation will always have a great influence on corporate effectiveness, especially in small firms (which have fewer points of leverage internally and less influence in the marketplace than larger companies), it behooves managers of smaller firms to become well versed in that knowledge.

A definition of what constitutes a smaller firm is needed in the very beginning. In an earlier book, we used $25 million in sales to define the upper limit of small firms.* In this book we have arbitrarily raised the limit to $50 million—arbitrarily because there is no clear or commonly accepted boundary between smaller and larger firms. Many a company at the high end of the smaller business range given here, say $45 million, is smaller than a firm doing half that volume, while some companies doing close to $25 million are larger, in terms of number of employees, and more complex than those doing four times as much.

In the book we go into a number of matters which may seem peripheral to the subject of compensation, such as motivation and cultural trends. We feel justified in doing so because the mechanics and formulas of compensation cannot be used with good results

*Theodore Cohn and Roy A. Lindberg, *Survival & Growth: Management Strategies for the Small Firm* (New York: AMACOM, 1974).

without considerable understanding of many seemingly distant matters, including why people behave as they do and what people are currently allowing to affect their behavior.

We acknowledge the classic contributions of Graef S. Crystal's *Executive Compensation* and Robert E. Sibson's *Compensation* (both published by AMACOM) and are indebted to many of their concepts.

On the practical side, however, we have given a number of illustrations and case studies bearing on compensation planning from work with our clients. For the same reasons, we have addressed ourselves in the book to the questions on compensation most frequently asked of us by the people who are the most logical readers for the book—the owners and the financial and personnel officers of smaller companies.

THEODORE COHN
ROY A. LINDBERG

Contents

Compensating
Key Executives
in the Smaller Company

1

The Importance and Role of Compensation

BECAUSE compensation programs in business are often based on invalid hypotheses, this chapter aims to identify the common determinants of pay and to clear the ground for understanding how to build effective compensation programs.

WHAT EMPLOYEES GIVE IS STRONGLY INFLUENCED BY PAY

In our society a company functions because people will exchange their time, knowledge, skills, and efforts for money. That fact is controlling in the field of compensation. Among other things, it means that there is an implied contract between a company and its employees on what the employees will give the company for what they are paid, and when the employees perceive they are not being paid fairly and equitably, they will give less than their best. Convinced they are not being paid fairly, the most capable people sooner or later are likely to deprive the company of their skills altogether by leaving. Where compensation is used to the limits of its ability to stimulate performance, employees convinced of their worth are induced to give all they can.

Employees have an infinite range of resources to draw on for the firm, and what they give is what keeps you in business and determines your degree of success in it. If inferior reasons—such as building family wealth, employing family incompetents at high salaries, or buying employee competence as cheaply as you can—are put ahead of paying people well (that is, fairly and in accordance with their competence), the employees who are the mainstays of your firm's health will know it and will give you only of their time, withholding their knowledge and skills. When pay is inadequate for unacceptable reasons, employees will spend a significant portion of their skills and efforts deceiving you, or they will leave you for better rewards than they are receiving.

A second controlling fact in the area of compensation is that the quality of pay bears materially on organizational structure and size. The lean and smoothly functioning organization is possible only in the enterprise that uses pay skillfully, uses it to stimulate pride, initiative, and teamwork. A lean organization, an organization which is relatively small for the amount of business it does, is always preferable to a fat one, which, with its excessive task specialization, numbers of employees, layers of supervision, and controls, is forced by inadequate compensation on companies otherwise well run.

Companies that do not employ pay to focus the efforts of employees on the firms' objectives must use more to accomplish less. Compared to companies that are skillful in the art of compensation, they will watch employees more closely, check on progress more frequently, and substitute more elaborate procedures to see that initiative, flexibility, and customer service do not wither and die.

A third controlling fact is that compensation programs are instruments of competition. The effects of pay inevitably show up in the results achieved in the marketplace. An effective program can attract and keep sharp managers and cause them to search for and exploit every opportunity to improve their company's affairs. An ineffective program retains incompetent managers, creates con-fusion as to what they should spend their time on, fosters organiza-tional dysfunction and counterproductive behavior, and detracts from the firm's performance in the marketplace.

Make no mistake about it: Employees produce goods and services in accordance with the values they associate with their pay. Employees express their feelings about compensation in such things as product development, product quality, level of service, product costs, delivery timeliness, territorial coverage, quality of sales and sales service, and order processing. And because customers fill their needs in accordance with their perceived values, and the values operate through purchases or refusals to buy, the compensation of employees inevitably bears upon sales volume and profitability.

USING PAY CONSTRUCTIVELY

Paying people so as to encourage them to become and stay productive is one of the most demanding, critical tasks of management. One reason is that no compensation program stands alone. Each program is part of a firm's total system of management; each is both an expression of and an influence upon the effective philosophy of administration, the ways and methods, and the seminal attitudes at work in an enterprise.

Another reason why effective compensation is not easily arranged is that programs cannot be devised on a factual basis alone. In the first place, there are no universal principles of compensation or motivation upon which small businessmen can depend as sure or just guides except those which are legislated or are functions of the labor market (in our own practice we have found remarkably few guidelines with broad applicability and none with universal applicability save those which are or border upon being truisms). Second, to come anywhere near completely separating one employee's performance from that of all other employees is either impossible or far too costly to do. Third, a new compensation plan, to the degree it is different, soon alters (modifies behavior taking place in) the environment in which it is implemented, thus adding a dimension of instability to the whole picture. For these reasons it is not possible to design a compensation program that is completely based on facts or entirely free of management's prejudices (which are, at their best, positive and constructive).

Another source of difficulty is that compensation plans *always* exist. The discourse that surrounds pay usually presumes that "a plan does not exist" or "we ought to have a plan." But the truth is

every enterprise has a compensation plan: At every moment in every
company, commitments are at work determining the pay of employees and how they are paid. It then follows that changes in
compensation practices (introducing a new plan) must overcome the
usual resistance to change. Resistance to changes affecting pay
particularly is to be minded because all such changes, except those
made "across the board," alter pay relationships (one's pay as
compared with another's), and that alone can be a major source of
organization-wracking problems.

In smaller companies a special source of difficulty is that
compensation planning tends to be episodic and performed by
nonspecialists. In almost all large firms the function has been
institutionalized and is performed on a continuing basis by well-
informed people. But smaller firms usually start to attend to
compensation only when forced to by the prospects of losing key
people or the need to secure additional staff to cope with rapid
growth. Even then, systematic compensation planning does not
always follow. The demands of key people are usually met without
attending to the compensation program as a totality, and the
problems of growth are usually met on a short-sighted, patchwork
basis.

Because smaller firms often grow much more quickly, proportionately, than large companies, during growth periods pay tends to
receive far less attention than the factors producing or the pangs
resulting from growth. The result, usually, is that new compensation
programs are conceived in haste, perpetuating the tatterdemalion
character of the pay program.

The magnitude of the compensation problem is indicated by the
difficulty of nailing down the language involved. Try to define some
of the words used so far and you will see how hard it is to be precise.
What do "being paid fairly and equitably," "performance," and even
"pay" mean?

Certainly "pay" does not mean the same thing to everyone.
Among other things, pay is what an employee thinks it is. If he thinks
it is his net weekly paycheck, it is; if it includes fringe benefits and he
is aware of them, that's his pay; and if it includes some of the
qualitative aspects of his work—such as the challenge of his job, the
conditions under which he works, his relations with his boss, the
friendships he has developed, his pride in the company—then those,
too, are part of his pay. On the other hand, to the extent that the

elements of pay are unrecognized by or are unclear to an employee, the dollars paid miss their mark. *Pay is what its receiver perceives it to be.*

Such considerations make it clear that there are no easy solutions to compensation problems. The plans in most smaller companies are usually makeshift and misdirected. To be made productive for employees *and* the company takes sure knowledge of where the firm should be headed, common sense, negotiation, courage, a sizable dose of selflessness, and the ability to live with uncertainty.

FOUR SOLUTIONS GUARANTEED TO CAUSE TROUBLE

Because of the confusion and hard work attending compensation planning, few smaller firms have rational compensation programs based on knowledge of their own corporate dynamics, practices in their industry, and social currents in the outside world. Compensation in most smaller firms is determined by something along the lines of the following convenient, undemanding, and usually unacknowledged methods.

The peace prize. Pay is used as a pacifier. The implied philosophy is: People can be paid to keep quiet. The approach can buy peace for a while but almost certainly will turn off key people. Worst of all, offered too often, it drives away the most essential of employees—the gifted manager.

The concept is essentially cost-related: How small a raise can we get away with? Usually some sensitivity to individual needs is displayed as window dressing, but the approach is basically unselective and does not address itself to the basic objectives of progressive compensation planning.

The hazy compromise. Do nothing unless you are forced to. When employees get restless, go through the motions of negotiating salary increases before giving in. A favorite tactic of managers who really don't know which executives are productive, the compromise muddies up any question about the relationship between performance and reward. Negotiations leave each employee clear only about the amount of his adjustment, but not *why* he was paid one amount rather than another, or what he can do to earn more. This differs from the "peace prize" solution in that it is employee-initiated and is calculated to be on the low side.

The suit off the rack. The manager uninterested in or incapable of developing a compensation program which is rational for his firm often adopts the plan of a company he thinks is comparable to his own. However, when he does so, he has the pay, motivational features, and limitations of the other firm. Lifting compensation programs from another company can be better than doing nothing at all, but it can lose a company the advantages of being different in some important way from competitors.

The best comparison we can make is with an apparel system which provides a size 50 suit to all grown males; no man will be arrested for indecency but few, if any, will look good.

The all-fitting copy system fails because each company is unique. The effective conditions of each firm's compensation are also unique. When a firm takes another's compensation program it will take in new problems without solving any of the old ones.

The revealed word. In this mode the basis of compensation lies in the mind of the chief executive. To appear both wise and fair, he reveals as little of his thinking as possible, thus guaranteeing that executive pay decisions not only are mysterious but cause dissension as well.

Even when the chief executive's motives are generous and benevolent, his decisions lack consistency, are bewildering to employees, and cannot really be defended. The approach ensures that employees will have no idea why they earned what they did and how they must change their performance in the future to earn more.

Any firm following one of these or similarly simplistic approaches is missing the appreciable benefits of a compensation plan tailored to its needs—needs which *always* include those of its employees.

WHAT COMPENSATION PLANNING CAN AND CANNOT DO

Like any management resource or tool, compensation has limitations. It will be useful at this point to see what compensation planning can be used to achieve and what it cannot. In reading the following lists, do not confuse *can* and *cannot do* with what compensation planning is sometimes *made* to do. Factually, compensation can be bent to almost any purpose. The capabilities and limitations cited below are those of effective compensation plans.

An effective compensation plan can assure a firm and its employees the following:

1. Pay which compares with that offered for similar positions in the job market.
2. Pay which accords with the demands and level of responsibility of a job internally.
3. Protection against the exigencies of life to the extent it can be afforded by the company.
4. Proper relationships between the base compensation given for standard performance in jobs at different levels.
5. Rewards for exceptional performance in proportion to the importance of the contribution.
6. Proper recognition of nonperformance factors such as inflation, tenure, total years of employment, etc.
7. Incentive for good performers to stay with the firm and contribute experience and knowledge.
8. Prevention of variable costs being transformed into fixed costs.
9. Pressure against the rise of unit costs of production and transactions.
10. Incentive and opportunity to grow as a person and a manager.

A compensation plan cannot do the following things:

1. Resolve conflicts between individual and corporate goals.
2. Determine the relative value of different jobs to the firm (that must be done by objective job evaluation).
3. Provide the basis for appraising performance (although it can specify *how* outstanding performance should be rewarded).
4. Establish what constitutes a job done acceptably or better (that is determined by position analysis and standards of performance).

INADEQUACY OF MOST GUIDELINES

Every compensation plan reflects convictions, implicit or otherwise, well founded or prejudiced, about such matters as why people work, what forms of compensation they want, and how pay affects productivity. However, most of the convictions are half-truths or baseless. They are formed in ignorance either of the facts of the environment in which the convictions are operative or of the research from which they originally sprang. Even well-based convictions are not always useful.

The research on employee behavior at work and the factors bearing on that behavior is extensive; but from the compensation viewpoint it offers either generalities too broad to be helpful in many situations or specifics too narrow to be helpful in more than a few. As a result, even the best-intentioned planning efforts come under the influence of principles which are suspect as to validity or motivational value. Examples of such follow:

□ Pay and performance are directly related; the more you pay people, the more they will produce.
□ The relationship between pay and performance is not the same for all employees or employee groups.
□ How people behave, perform, produce can be changed by changing the way they are paid.
□ Pay is only one of the factors influencing motivation and performance.
□ Incentives are the best way to improve performance.

Not one of the foregoing has universal validity. Each proposition is true in given situations but false in others. The first point illustrates the limitations of the generalizations, for although common experience and studies of the subject show that pay and performance often go hand in hand, we cannot say with certainty: Pay this and get that. True, where the chance to earn more money realistically exists, increased efforts and improved results often follow. But not always, because increased pay is not the leading objective of every employee, and even among those for whom it is, pay is defined and viewed differently.

Pay is not the only factor affecting performance, and it is deadly to compensation planning to presume otherwise. Even with high compensation, an employee may still not become or stay a high performer (any more than he fails to be a high performer because of low pay). Repetitive, boring work, too long hours, internal dissension, unabated pressure, lack of acceptance by his peers, and, of course, private emotional problems may bear more on his efforts than pay.

Similarly, even when the pay reward system does affect how people behave and use their time, it does not necessarily follow that the directions taken help the business. Not all companies create clear understanding of what is wanted of employees, nor are employees always primarily concerned with improving the company's operations or profits. Many are so interested in "doing their own thing," enjoying particular kinds of work, having job security, or working free of tension that the opportunities for more money take second or third place.

Guidelines in the form of theories, concepts, principles, and so forth are essential, but they cannot take the place of or be used safely without the support of facts. Before you can use the generally available compensation guidelines productively, you need to have a great variety and amount of specific information. Among other things, you need to know how your people feel about the company, their work, and their performance, what their career aspirations are, what their potentials for growth are, what their interests in life are, and what the prospects for your business are. In the absence of such knowledge, guidelines can cause more harm than good.

OUR PREMISES

Since compensation planning cannot be totally free of subjective influences, you should be aware of some of the premises which underlie the views expressed in these pages about compensation. These premises are as follows:

Success in Business Is Largely Rational

Long hours and good luck may be followed by business success, but the companies which have survived and prospered are those in which management has worked hard at determining on an informed basis such things as what the company should be doing, how it should be organized, and how people should be paid for producing what results.

To say that success in business is completely rational is unrealistic in a world which is considerably irrational. However, our own experience and a good deal of other evidence show that things are usually more integrated than surface appearances indicate. For example, the moral and ethical values which permeate a firm can influence its internal and total environment in major ways and, therefore, factor significantly in the firm's success.

The world is less or more rational (that is, comprehensible and responsive) depending upon the amount of knowledge we possess and bring to bear upon it, and the intelligence with which we substitute for the knowledge we do not possess. Thus, the relationship between what we expect and what we get from compensation depends upon the amount of knowledge and the quality of assumptions employed in the compensation plans laid.

Corporate Rationality Hinges on Decision Quality

Objectives, however clear and worthy, cannot be achieved in a firm where special pains are not taken to assure sound decision making. The best compensation planning in the world will not direct employees against the forces that permit, foster, and insist upon inferior decision making. Objective, corporate-serving decision making is absolutely required for compensation programs to work effectively.

The sequence in which major decisions are made in a firm bears considerably on their quality. As we see it, the sequence in decision making should be:

1. How will the decision affect the firm's survival (retention of assets)?

2. How will the decision affect the firm's liquidity (ability to pay its bills)?

3. How will the decision affect profits or profitability (present and/or future)?

If the answer to any of the three is negative—that is, the decision will impair or not enhance the firm's survivability, liquidity, or profitability—in a healthy firm the decision ought not be made at all. In a firm on the way to bankruptcy, a negative answer in the decision line does not necessarily rule out making a decision; in a firm whose survival requires the taking of a massive risk, the sequence is irrelevant.

Assessment of the risks involved in decision making should be similarly conducted. For example, the first question to be asked when taking on a new venture committing the company to a new or untried area of a market is not "how much can we make?" but "how much can we afford to lose?" The question of how much we can make does not touch upon the firm's ability to survive or hold on to its assets. Determining how much we may lose, on the other hand, may lead to the disclosure that we are gambling with the survival of the company. Again, no venture should be undertaken which risks the firm's survival except by a firm whose survival in any case is at stake.

The main difficulty in decision making is in assessing what constitutes a realistic contribution to a firm's health or growth. It is not unusual for what appear to be innovative, profit-building ventures to turn out to be potentially or actually disastrous upon further analysis or the passage of time. Observing the foregoing decision-making sequence and turning the decision question around helps distinguish contribution from noncontribution.

Employees Control Their Output

Companies in our society can exist because employees exchange nonmonetary commodities (their time, interest, skill, creativity) for money. Therefore, employees, not management, control their output, in part, according to what they are paid. The extent of the resources which employees contribute to the firm is also partly determined by management's motives in compensation. It is impossible to hide such motives for long; if they are inferior, the employees will know it and give only of their time, not their higher capabilities. Because compensation affects the kind of commitments an employee chooses to make, it ultimately bears upon sales volume and profitability. Harvey Leibenstein* has shown how the risk-reward system works to reduce employees' willingness to take initiative and challenge existing procedures. In most companies, the punishment for failure is greater than the reward for success. Since an employee's survival (keeping the job, avoiding criticism, not being disturbed) is a higher priority than increasing his employer's profits, he protects himself by not taking risks. Compensation for successful risk taking can go far toward expanding employees' involvement and creativity.

A Company Does Not Make Money by Paying as Little as Possible

The general population views businessmen as masters of the art

---

*Beyond Economic Man: A New Approach to Micro-Economic Theory (Cambridge, Mass.: Harvard University Press, 1976).

of paying as little as possible for the work they get out of people. To be sure, some managers operate on that principle, particularly in small, newly established firms. But high-performing companies do not operate that way. Such companies believe in the aphorism "human resources are the most important of all" and do not stint on compensation. They pay for the best, and pay to keep them best.

Compensation Planning Is a Form of Cost Control

Despite the implications likely to be drawn from the preceding idea, the main benefit to be sought from compensation planning is lowered cost of doing business. True, to achieve that on anything near a durable basis will require many prior achievements, such as the development of clear and worthy objectives, personal satisfaction with pay, and a goal-focused reward system. But just as employee happiness is not the chief reason a company is in business, so making people happy with their earnings is not the chief reason behind compensation planning. The reasons are to lower the cost of purchasing, production, transactions, sales, or shipping and to increase the competitive product or service advantages which bear on the firm's prosperity and prospects.

Each·Successful Company Is Unique

Each sound, financially healthy firm operates imaginatively and uniquely in its environment, its markets. It is run from the outside in, from the viewpoint of fulfillment of customer needs, with the intention of providing benefits to purchasers superior to those attainable elsewhere, with sensitivity to changing customer needs, with the objective of building durable relations, and so forth. The company that is run that way is not the same as others, nor merely what the owners or key managers want it to be. What sets it apart from other firms also constitutes its competitive advantages.

The significance of uniqueness from the viewpoint of compensation is that if a company can identify what it does uniquely, what sets it apart, it can then create the jobs *and the reward system* that will increase the chances that its superiorities will continue. In other words, once it knows its advantages and the type of performance it wants, it can then better tie together organizational and personal goals. *Pay* provides a good deal of the cordage for tying the two together.

There is another aspect to the concept of each company's

developing its own tailor-made compensation program, that is, the creation of a compensation plan which in itself is competitively different and superior. A compensation plan can be a competitive tool to a company that attracts and retains employees who are abler or more clearly directed than those hired by competitors.

Example. In an industry in which salespersons were paid a flat percentage of gross profit (usually 50 percent), two entrepreneurs developed a compensation system which allowed top salespersons to earn as much as 82 percent of the gross margin. The owners had computed that once a salesperson's gross profit dollars had covered the largely fixed costs of handling his sales orders, almost all the additional margin was profit. By allocating budgeted costs and a reasonable share of corporate profit to each salesperson, the owners were able to offer sales commissions dramatically more attractive than those of competitors. Within three years they had a stable of 15 salespersons who were hungry to take advantage of the opportunity to earn large incomes.

Later, in Chapter 4, we will develop a simple model in which the company's uniqueness can be identified and the integration of the company's jobs, information, decision making, reward system, and controls can be described.

Smaller Companies Are Different from Large Companies

Smaller companies are not merely shrunken versions of large ones but are substantively different in many ways. For example, they have more conservative accounting, and their reported taxable profits are usually less because of the need to retain earnings and the desire of owners to avoid dividends through tax-deductible ways of taking money out of the company. Smaller companies are also freer than large companies to be creative about compensation, to devise programs more responsive to the needs and interests of their top managers *and* of their companies.

People Make the Difference in Successful Companies

Materials, machinery, money, and even methods tend to be nondifferentiating, but how companies choose and use personnel tends to set them apart. Companies that employ human resources in a distinctive way usually are innovative in compensation planning. Among other things, they usually have exploited the advantages smaller firms have over large firms by offering an atmosphere in which contributing individuals can feel important and where some basic social and psychological needs can be satisfied in a healthy, nonmanipulative way. The compensation plans of such companies are designed to make the best use of the firm's human resources, an absolute requirement to earning the best results.

The Time of the Top Managers Is a Firm's Largest Unrecorded Asset

Usually few people, rarely more than half a dozen, create the leverage factors in smaller companies (except, perhaps, in professional firms). How these people spend their time greatly influences the results achieved in successful firms. A large percentage of the time of top managers in successful firms is spent in working in the key areas that can enhance or introduce corporate advantages. The reward system in such firms encourages that behavior.

Therefore, compensation programs should be designed to make clear to everyone that the protection, exploitation, and enhancement of the firm's unique qualities, its competitive advantages, will be specially rewarded. Pay will then have a disproportionately salutary effect on the use of time and the results achieved.

The Outside World Has the Ultimate Influence Over the Affairs of a Company

The better the management of a company becomes, the more sensitive it is to the influence the environment has on the firm. A successful firm becomes increasingly responsive to what is going on in the part of the world it is supplied by, sells to, collects from. It is hard under any condition to define, stay in touch with, and react to that world. Smaller companies particularly need to set aside time and money to find out what is going on in it, and to prepare to profit from the changes taking place. The most successful companies work the hardest at becoming and remaining conversant with the outside world.

Unable to support the full-time expertise of the large company, the smaller company that stands out consciously identifies and marshals its resources for knowing what is going on in the outside world, and accepts the limitations of its internal resources. It overcomes them by using every available type of outside help. The kinds of help available are not only at cost, such as that provided by consultants, industrial psychologists, engineers, CPA's, attorneys, outside board or executive committee members, but are also free of cost, such as that provided by insurance agents, government agencies, and industrial associations.

When outside influences rather than managerial skill determine profits, a compensation system aimed at directing management effort is probably wasted. It is more important to identify correctly the outside influence and make the proper response.

Example. After a gradual sales decline a small chain of restaurants in downtown locations started losing money. An incentive plan for the restaurant managers failed to turn the tide. A new financial vice-president analyzed marginal income and then turned to the outside world for an explanation of location profitability. He identified successful restaurants from location and traffic patterns rather than individual management talent.

The incentive compensation plan was therefore irrelevant. The company needed a real estate expert more than improved restaurant operating talent. After the president was convinced that the outside world impact was the primary influence on the firm, he hired a real estate manager, dropped the incentive compensation plan, and as normal turnover took place, replaced the local restaurant managers with lower-salaried people.

There Are No Simple Compensation Answers

The foregoing premises make it obvious that there are no single answers to the similar problems of different companies or simple answers to complex problems within a company. Therefore, a simple compensation program is almost sure to fail.

Smaller-business managers have looked for simple solutions for many years. They have tried everything from human relations training and budgeting, management by objectives (MBO), computers, long-range planning, and cash-forecasting to transactional analysis, transcendental meditation, group therapy, yoga, yogurt, jogging, tennis, and other mystical solutions to business problems. Some techniques or methods have helped some individual managers and companies; others are obviously fads and frauds.

Though each technique may have chipped away at some management or operating problems, no single business technique will solve many of your problems or all of a major problem.

Compensation Planning Is Not a Cure-All

Few real problems in business can be solved simply by changing the compensation plan. The role played by compensation in solving business problems is important, but it is not *the* answer. While it is true that many business problems cannot be solved without dealing with pay, it is also true that dealing with pay alone will rarely cure a business problem. Compensation problems always have noncompensation components.

A corollary is that defective compensation planning has some of its roots elsewhere. And if deficiencies other than pay have to be dealt with also, compensation planning will go awry again and again.

COMPENSATION QUESTIONS TYPICALLY ASKED

The following questions, culled from those asked at the many seminars we have run, indicate the common problems of compensation and their complexity:

1. Do small companies (say $4 to $5 million annual sales) need formal wage administration programs? If not, at what size should such programs be considered?
2. What are the mechanics of administering such a program? What are the key things we should include?
3. Where do I find salary ranges against which to measure what I'm paying my top managers?
4. What is fair pay for a chief executive officer (CEO) in a profitable, closely held company with sales of $5-$10 million, $10-$20 million, $20-$50 million?
5. What compensation plan can we set up for nonstockholder-managers based on the gross profit they produce less the indirect controllable expenses?
6. Can pay be used to modify the performance of a person greedy for power or a person who needs constant support?
7. Our compensation plan, which was heavily weighted toward profit, worked well when business was good, but it has been a disaster in recession periods. How do you cover such differences in the business cycle?
8. What can we do about compression of wages, that is, the effect of higher lower-level starting salaries on our management-level salaries?

9. How do we get out of a bad compensation deal, one that seemed right when we started but is now wrong?

10. Do managers work twice as hard with the promise of twice as much pay?

11. Should managers' bonuses be limited to a specific percentage of base salary (when the earnings produced by the same managers responsible are not)?

12. How can we set up objectives and then measure the qualitative aspects of a job so that we can tie financial rewards to the job?

13. What are the key elements of a good cash incentive program?

14. Is there any way of convincing a foreign-owned parent corporation to follow local U.S. compensation policies which vary from the European models?

15. What arguments can be marshaled against an IRS charge that a top executive salary is unreasonable?

16. What formulas can separate compensation for stock ownership, job responsibility, and specific performance in the closely held company where the payment of dividends is considered a poor tax policy?

17. How do you handle an extraordinary performer in a background of corporate loss or breakeven?

18. How do you separate individual and group pay so that the executive does not make money to the detriment of the company? (For instance, he gets paid when his department does well but the company does poorly, perhaps as the result of his success.)

19. When sales are slow and salespeople are earning less than they have become accustomed to, what type of encouragement—compensation or otherwise—can you offer them to do better?

20. If salespeople are paid on gross margin, is it better to set a minimum percentage and pay commission as soon as the order is booked, or wait until the end of the month and pay on the overall gross margin?

21. Is there a simple sales compensation program which covers both commissions and expenses in one package?

22. How do you convince an outside board of directors who are

majority stockholders about the validity of a return on assets (ROA) method of executive compensation?

23. Should a bonus be directed to individuals rather than group-oriented, whether it is based on return on assets (ROA) or profit?

24. Is there some salary level at which compensation aside from cash should be used?

25. Must the management-team approach to compensation reduce payments for different levels of performance of team members and therefore act as a demotivator?

26. What is the role of compensation with a management team which appears to be self-motivated, that is, more concerned with corporate performance and self-actualization than money?

27. In a successful growth company, how do you determine whether you are paying too much or too little to your management team as a group?

28. Should managerial salaries be increased automatically as cost-of-living increases take place? Similarly, if we have a devaluation, should salaries be tied to the value of the dollar?

29. We are considering dropping our annual Christmas bonus, which is related directly to salaries, and establishing a company profit-sharing plan. Do you think this is a good idea?

30. How do you handle the pay of nonunion people when business is bad but union employees receive increased wages through their negotiated contracts?

31. How do you attract, retain, and satisfy top-level, nonfamily executives in a family-owned company dominated by owner-managers?

32. How do you transfer significant pieces of ownership to young managers who do not have enough money to buy stock? Our intent is to give or sell them enough ownership and interest to retain them for eventual takeover.

33. Below the owner/president level, how do you establish an equitable compensation program for first-line managers?

34. What is new in compensation? Are there any ideas that worked well in the past but don't work now?

35. How do you reward really superior performance?

36. What fringes give you the most return for your money? What are the most effective noncash incentives?
37. How do you answer the executive who asks, "What do I have to do here to earn a lot more money?"
38. It is relatively easy to determine the contribution of sales-people. What criteria are there for measuring the performance of service, administrative, and staff managers?
39. How far can fringe benefits such as cars and club memberships go without raising IRS questions?

Once you have cleared the planning foundation of the debris of false assumptions and prejudices affecting pay and have formulated a set of hypotheses, you are ready to get on with the job of compensation planning. Guidelines to the formulation of effective compensation plans follow in the next chapter.

2

Guidelines to Effective Compensation Planning

IN this chapter we examine the potentials of the compensation function to contribute to the achievement of a firm's objectives and present guidelines useful in designing any compensation program.

ASPECTS OF MANAGING INFLUENCED BY COMPENSATION

With some risk of oversimplification, let us examine each of the main business activities to see where compensation can influence outcomes.

What markets, products, and/or services are to be offered?

At this point in the managerial process compensation is not significant. The selection of markets to be served is primarily influenced by opportunity factors and capital availability, not by what it would cost to have the *kinds* of skills and performance that would enable the selections to work.

What must be done to succeed in the markets selected?

At this level of strategy selection, compensation is a consideration, but it is not determining. More relevant are the work which must be done, the numbers of people needed to do the work, and the organizational structure needed.

What types of people do we need?

When it comes to attracting, hiring, training, and retaining the kinds of people (those who have the skills plus the interest and ability to contribute) needed for the company to succeed in the markets selected, compensation gains its first major importance. The quality of the compensation program used will determine substantially the caliber of people you can attract and retain.

How do we achieve the results we want?

Here compensation has maximum leverage. How we stimulate our people to operate to the outer edges of their capacities, which performance factors we watch, will depend on the reward system chosen. What you will get from your top people is substantially related to the kinds and qualities of incentives and rewards you offer as long as they are consistent with other basic management philosophy and practices.

THE FIRST AMONG PLANNING GUIDELINES

The greatest influence compensation can have is on the actions taken to realize the objectives and strategies of a firm. At its best, compensation is an instrument for making things happen. Therefore, the first among the guidelines to compensation planning is: *Design your compensation plan to get your people to put fulfillment of the company goals and objectives first.* Make sure your compensation plan does not contradict your company's goals.

To make compensation effective, the goals and objectives of the firm must be explicit, clear, and acceptable. That is a big job, one that usually looks too big to most managers in small companies. But it is one that must be done if compensation planning is to return its costs. If you cannot find, generate, bring out into the open fundamental and agreeable goals and objectives, don't bother to plan compensation. Just keep patching up the old system—it will be good enough.

THE OTHER GUIDELINES

Many other actions at the practical level are required after the setting of worthy corporate goals to realize the prime objectives of compensation planning. Guidelines for realizing these objectives follow.

Attract the right number and kinds of managers
Each compensation program should be devised to attract good people. Even when you think you are well and fully staffed, designing your program so that the salaries are attractive to competent outsiders will be of benefit. Among other things, it will constitute one more check that you are paying your present people correctly.

In order to satisfy this objective you will have to know what competitive salary levels are, what good people want out of work, and the forms of compensation that are attractive to them.

Keep the good performers
Next, the program should be designed to retain the firm's good performers and to make the company unattractive to the firm's inadequate or mediocre managers.

Raise performance to outer limits
Compensation should be planned to motivate, to encourage people to perform at high levels. An effective compensation policy directs people's behavior toward the quality of work and results that will help the enterprise reach its goals.

However, be careful of falling into the trap of thinking that more money necessarily will raise performance. Money *alone* seldom raises the performance of those who matter. True, there is some relationship between high performance and monetary satisfaction on the job, but happiness on the job for all but the exceptional is usually more related to retention than performance.

If pay will not affect performance and profits, then there is usually very little reason to change pay.

Example. A retail chain of 15 stores paid its managers salaries which were low but reasonable in the small towns in which they lived.

Concerned with the overall low profitability of the chain, the chief executive officer (CEO) investigated the possibility of raising the pay and bonus of the individual store managers. Upon analysis, it was clear that the factors that caused profitability—such as location, merchandising policy, pricing, advertising, and a competitive inventory level—were not under the manager's direction. Under those conditions, raising store managers' pay would not materially improve store profitability.

The analysis showed that corporate profits were affected by decisions made at the executive level, to which the CEO should direct his attention to develop performance standards and rewards.

Pay for results

The most successful compensation programs pay for results, not activities, for outputs, not inputs. They give proper weight to individual and group contributions, and differentiate sufficiently between routine and extraordinary performance so that the outstanding performer (the person you should be most interested in) is rewarded proportionately. Because all these factors are difficult to determine and fit into a compensation program, we will deal with them in more detail (see Chapter 3).

People whose work is challenging are likely to be satisfied. But people who are happy are not necessarily productive. If pay cannot affect profits and performance, don't change pay (except for nonperformance-related factors such as rises in the cost of living).

Keep the firm competitive

Minimally, effective compensation plans maintain a firm's competitive ability by not putting it at a competitive disadvantage. However, compensation not only attracts and retains the employees you want; it also makes them affordable. Since compensation is usually the first or second largest cost in operating a company, pay levels should be competitive.

To make compensation competitively meaningful (in all cases except where survival calls for sacrifice), you have to match salaries paid for equivalent positions in your employment areas, particularly those paid by competitors. On the other hand, you must also be prepared to lose someone whose salary demands are so great that they fall outside the upper limits of reasonableness.

Almost every firm, especially those with minimum growth opportunities, will be faced with losing an executive whose salary

demand is greater than your evaluation and local wage levels justify.
A company in another area or under pressure to fill a position
quickly will be able to satisfy the executive's demands. If your
evaluation and salary-level procedures are working, these situations
should be rare.

Protect stockholders' investment

Effective compensation plans do not threaten the sources or
quality of employment of capital; before any other considerations
they require a fair return to stockholders. The return should not
only cover the cost of capital but also protect capital against future
risks and uncertainties, including inflation. What constitutes a
reasonable pretax rate of return before bonus distribution of the
excess varies with the industry and each company's history and plans.

Be seen as fair

A compensation plan cannot be effective if it is not seen as fair
and achievable with opportunities and clear definitions of what must
be done to earn more. Most people make judgments about their
compensation with inadequate knowledge, because they rarely know
what other people do and usually lack the information needed to
compare their performances with others, especially when they are
working in parallel. Managers of stores, departments that do not
impinge on each other, design engineers working on different
projects, accountants and lawyers working for different clients—all
have inadequate exposure to the work of others and are therefore ill
equipped to evaluate. Nevertheless, they make the comparisons.
Therefore, a compensation policy which is not seen as fair will
probably demotivate those people who have the highest responsibilities, take the biggest risks, and produce the most for the
company.

Employees, especially those with a sense of worth, also make
comparisons between their pay and what is paid for jobs they think
they can fill in other organizations. That does not necessarily show
they are looking to change; it indicates that one of the recognized
measures of their worth is their comparative earnings.

Employees with a sense of worth want their self-evaluation
corroborated. They want to feel they are not being exploited; they
want to be able to say: "In this area in this type of job I am worth
$___ to $___ and I'm in that range." Good people are extremely
conscious of what others with equivalent responsibilities earn, and

expect to be paid at least what competition in the same industry and in the same area offers. Consciously or unconsciously they are constantly scanning the compensation horizon. They check newspapers, industry journals, and trade associations and compare salaries with associates at professional meetings, alumni clubs, and the like.

Managers should explore and jointly plan the pay programs with key people to get their reactions and suggestions before resolving the philosophy and the details. It is arrogant to impose a compensation program, especially an incentive plan, from above without first testing its reasonableness with those involved.

Meet the varying needs of employees

People don't want the same things out of life, and it is therefore unrealistic to expect they want the same things out of compensation. An effective compensation plan takes into account that people's needs differ in accordance with their individual situations and perspectives.

Age, family size, education, and health are factors which affect amounts and character of the income needs of employees. Within the bounds of fairness, sound compensation planning is tailored to individual needs.

Pay special attention to the needs of key people

The success of most firms depends upon a handful of gifted, extraordinarily motivated people. Good compensation planning makes special provision for them.

Performance should be separated at different levels of contribution. If you do not want to evaluate and pay for outstanding output, then you may as well pay for seniority, charm, looks, height, weight, punctuality, straight sales commissions, blood relationship, or anything except a real evaluation.

If you cannot identify exceptional performance and pay accordingly, you will turn off the key people in the organization. It is not part of their nature to be lumped—in terms of pay or other forms of recognition and reward—with run-of-the-mill producers. Because of their importance to the firm, it is advisable to periodically arrive at fresh judgments as to the adequacy of key employees' pay and to adjust the compensation plan as the judgments indicate.

Key employees, high in the organization or with a skill in demand in the world, are generally more aware of salary levels outside the company than within. A manager setting up and administering a pay system should constantly monitor the salaries, including the total fringe benefit package, of those groups with whom his key people are likely to be comparing their pay.

Small company managers who lose key people to larger competitors find convenient the excuse that the employee left solely for money. Although large companies reach out for desirable employees with financial inducements, salary differences mask basic dissatisfactions with the type of work, opportunity for advancement, and inability to become a stockholder or have a say in major decisions in a closed organization. We can accept salary difference as the reason for leaving more readily than the other reasons, which suggest managerial inadequacy.

Differences in fringe benefits rarely cause turnover; when an employee feels they are unfair, he may be resentful. But do not expect improved performance should you correct the inequities by giving the same insurance, vacation, and retirement benefits as others. Usually, you do no more than eliminate one source of discontent.

Poor or unfair administration of a pay system is an increasing source of turnover the higher the level of competence involved. An evaluation system insensitive or blind to both real and perceived significant differences in performance evaluation and pay will ultimately force key people to leave.

Focus attention on work

A major objective of compensation planning should be to keep employees' eyes on their work rather than on their pay, which requires that the plan be designed to create enough satisfaction with earnings so that nonmonetary motives can come to the fore. A compensation plan founded on the assumption that pay is the only motivating force will be self-defeating. Such plans usually stimulate self-serving behavior and provide a skimpy foundation for the production of corporate gains or sustained work satisfaction. If money alone is used to change behavior, then only *more* money will have the power to change behavior.

Keep options open

A well-designed compensation plan does not lock a firm into the features of the design or become the basis of pay traditions. Well-run companies are willing and quick to change their plans as they learn more about their key people, the relationships between pay and performance, and competitive compensation practices. You should not take the risk of letting a competitor outrun you because it has a more flexible and sensitive compensation system.

Skilled managers tend to be experimental in designing their compensation plans. A group of the largest professional organizations in the world changes their partners' evaluation and pay programs almost annually. This is not weakness or indecisiveness—it is a sign that pay is too important to be frozen.

FACTORS FROM THE EXTERNAL ENVIRONMENT

In shaping compensation policy and plans you should take into account factors in both the economic and social world. A discussion of some of these factors follows.

De-emphasis on growth
A slowing down of U.S. economic growth and rising questions globally of the desirability of growth have increased the value of job security as opposed to career growth.

Rising incidence of family employment
The percentage of women working and the number of families with two or more wage earners are increasing. More families are considering the careers of all those working and are less willing to accept promotion opportunities if they require relocation or are likely to have a negative effect on family life.

Increasing professionalism at higher work levels
Professionals want to negotiate their pay and are less willing to accept arbitrary decisions on what they are worth. The definition of a professional has expanded beyond the traditional designations of lawyer, engineer, or accountant to include the young manager who sees his loyalty primarily to himself and the work he is doing.

The expanded definition may include a cost or budget expert, sales manager, draftsman, warehouse supervisor, computer programmer, and anyone else who sees his work, his pay, and his lifestyle as inseparable.

The onset of permanent inflation
Inflation has become an integral part of base pay. Few companies do not routinely raise their salary levels and, in many cases, their merit pay to match inflation.

Inflation more than real growth has been the source of growth in revenue, and the better compensation managers adjust both sales and return on investment as measures of performance because of inflation. Some have turned to sales units or have built in a de-inflation factor when relating bonuses to sales volume.

The trend toward individualism

Most working groups are moving away from group thinking, but the movement toward individualism has been most pronounced among bright, youthful male and female executives.

The development of unemployment protection programs has helped to shift people's priorities from fear of not being able to earn a living to a concern for doing what one prefers to do. The result has been that even persons of ordinary gifts now have choices in terms of jobs, lifestyles, and places to live that were before available only to the select few. The sophisticated young manager entering business is conscious of the possible conflict between what he wants out of his life and what being successful in corporate terms demands. He often resolves the conflict in favor of his lifestyle.

Such issues as the following have been raised:

"How much loyalty do I owe a company if it won't allow me to be loyal to my own beliefs?"

"We are what we make of ourselves when we compromise our code of ethics, our integrity, and when we steal from society."

In an article called "Here Come the Individualists," Louis Banks made the following statements which highlight the fact that compensation does not stand alone, but is one of the tools by which young, bright workers and managers can be attracted, retained, and motivated in their work:

> An enlightened corporation (unlike the army, civil service, and some religious orders) wants its people to enjoy themselves, to seize responsibility, to think new thoughts. It pays them well and takes care of them in sickness and old age. . . . A good corporation is a rather civilized institution.
>
> The corporation's role has become so central that it is there that modern man turns for satisfaction of the security, justice, and esteem needs.*

Harvard Magazine, Sept.–Oct. 1977.

It seems to us that, with the decline of other institutions and the significant time spent by managers at their work, these statements have a very solid basis. Most of us have little contact with the law, and our sense of justice is likely to be determined more by the opportunities we are given and the basis on which rewards are distributed at work than by some abstract sense of justice.

Once we pass the subsistence level represented by unemployment benefits, welfare, and Social Security, our sense of security is also determined by how our employer treats us and by the economic success of his enterprise. In other words, job security can be shown to be directly proportionate to the results attained by an employer. This coincidence of goals is one of the obvious strengths of any compensation policy.

MYTHS AND FACTS ABOUT EXECUTIVE COMPENSATION

Abraham K. Korman of BFS Psychological Associates, Inc., New York City, has put together the following list* of myths and facts about executive compensation, consideration of which offers a useful way of connecting some of the current findings of behavioral science relating to performance and pay.

If the position has opportunity for achievement and growth, money becomes less important
According to Korman, this is a myth. He says money is important, stands on its own, and cannot be downgraded by trying to offset it with opportunities for professional achievement or growth.

We agree. We live in a world of rising expectations. Money is wanted as much as the intangibles; they are not trade-offs. New ventures, new projects, difficult problem solving all stand to fail if money is not among the rewards offered to the risk takers, the decision makers, the people who invest disproportionate effort to make things work.

Even the expression "doing your own thing" supports the "value" of money. Doing one's thing usually requires enough money from one's job to do it away from work as well as at it.

Rising expectations are one of the causes of job-hopping; the

*Reprinted with permission of Dr. Korman.

increasing mobility of competent executives is often motivated by the desire for more challenge as well as more money.

Younger executives are as interested in money as older executives

This seems to be a fact. The younger generation is oriented to the present. They have grown up in a period in which the future was both doubtful because of the potential of nuclear holocaust and assured because government provisions for ultimate security have made the need to have a job less important than it was 50 years ago. They are interested in current achievement, current growth, and they realize that money is one of the scorecards on which their professional success is measured. Younger executives do not want to have to pass up certain things they feel are important: cars, trips, clothes, other visible signs of achievement.

On the other hand, executives of 40 or older tend to realize that some things in life are more important than money and that there are certain significant values over which money has no influence. Money cannot return a dead parent, cannot repair many of life's disappointments, cannot create positive relations with children, cannot assure good health or long life. They have also seen that money put first can damage values and relationships. For older executives, money is still important, but for those who have enough—admittedly a highly subjective standard—it is seen more as a sign of success, of capability, of still being needed and wanted than as a thing of value for itself.

The bottom line is the only way to evaluate the performance of executives and to apportion rewards

This is probably a myth, says Korman, and we agree. No one denies the significance of the bottom line as a measure of performance, but it certainly is not the only measure, and when used alone, it can be tricky and deceptive.

Moreover, because it reflects past performance, it comes too late to direct (and correct) the efforts of executives. Managers who do not plan to stay with the company can distort the figures for a period. Consider the manager whose bonus is based on the bottom line of his department. He can reduce or eliminate expenditures that will affect only the future to show extraordinary results in the present. For example, he can drop all training, maintenance, repairs, and—if he has control of them—advertising, sales promotion, the level of sales service. The moves will benefit his bottom line, but harm the company's long-range health.

Using the bottom line (departmental or corporate) to evaluate performance has other limitations. It does not reflect many significant results for which executives are responsible and should be rewarded, such as the quality of relationships with vendors and customers, the development of managers, and the solving of major problems. And it fails to account for the effort, problems, and managerial growth which the manager may have experienced and are worthy of reward. The same result could have been reached by different routes which should be individually evaluated. These differences are not reflected in the income statement but inevitably affect future results.

The bottom line has to be made clear. For example, a bank offered a bonus for each $50 savings account that a teller opened. One teller persuaded a depositor with $500 to open ten accounts at $50 each. The additional cost wiped out the advantages to the bank. The strategy aimed at improving the bottom line did not prevent performance damaging to the bottom line.

In another case one of the major airlines created incentive programs for the station manager and the head of the baggage-handling department. The performance of the station manager was to be measured by the overall profitability of the station; the performance of the baggage-handling manager was measured by cost control only. It is not too difficult to see that these courses were on a collision path. The baggage-handling manager soon saw that his interest would be best served by eliminating any labor he could. The result was an extremely low cost ratio but one of the worst baggage-handling records in the United States. The station manager did not directly supervise the baggage-handling manager (who was under a regional baggage supervisor), and was powerless to change the system.

It did not take higher-level management long to realize that holding each manager to bottom-line results did not produce consistent results for the company. They then changed the system to provide for overall profitability and, in the case of the baggage-handling manager, set up a standard of service below which he received no bonus. Thereafter, his bottom-line goal became the same as that of the station manager.

We have stated that money is important to almost everyone and that there may be some, but by no means a linear, relationship between the offer of more money and the possibility of obtaining higher performance. However, we also know, even before we investigate the findings of behavioral sciences that apply to work, that many people work for reasons other than money. Therefore, if the bottom line becomes the sole basis of reward for performance, we can lose some of the other reasons for which people work.

If we emphasize the bottom line only and offer more for money as the sole reward, we lose or diminish the opportunities to help employees get more out of their work through job satisfaction and personal growth.

Compensation programs work better when pay is offered as a reward rather than as an incentive

The difference between a reward and an incentive is that a reward is made after the fact, whereas an incentive states in advance: "Do this and you will get that." Korman feels it is probably true that compensation works better as a reward than as an incentive. Managers have limited control over the people under them. External circumstances, competition, availability of product, inflation, and many gratuitous events affect the end results. Since managers have to make compromises with both their environments and their subordinates, they will look more favorably on compensation given as a reward than as an incentive.

Incentives are extremely hard to set for some managers since many performance elements are difficult to isolate or set standards for. It is hard to put down in advance what constitutes superior, acceptable, or unacceptable performance for someone whose main concern is purchasing or the more routine accounting functions.

However, our experience with hundreds of managers tells us that they are at a loss when they don't know what they have to do in order to gain recognition. With few exceptions, our interviews have shown that managers prefer to know *in advance* what they have to do to be judged superior, adequate, or inadequate. They also prefer to know as specifically as possible what the rewards will be for different levels of performance.

Everyone accepts the need to leave part of the distribution of rewards to discretion because of the impossibility of knowing in advance who will be faced with the toughest problems, what the future effects of present contributions will be, who will grow the most, and so forth. Given the choice between rewards or incentives, our experience is that most managers would prefer incentives.

In designing a compensation program, emphasize the amount that is likely to be made rather than the amount that can be made

This is a fact, says Korman, and we agree. Here we are dealing with the relationships between expectations and achievement. People are less likely to be disappointed if their money expectations are realistic. Moreover, managers are likely to be motivated to try harder to the degree the rewards are attainable (as well as worthwhile).

You should therefore emphasize, particularly in a new hiring situation, what an employee is *likely* to earn rather than the upper limit of what he *may* make if everything goes well. Unhappiness, disappointment, and demotivation come less frequently from the amount made than from failing to make what was hoped. These observations tie in with those of David C. McClelland of the Harvard Business School, whose pioneering studies of self-motivated achievers show marked falloff of effort when expectations are too high. Small-firm managers can individualize the career paths of their few key managers and avoid unrealistic expectations.

Women executives are less interested in money than male executives

We agree with Korman that this idea is a myth. Women at the same levels in an organization are as interested in money as men. We need not discuss the rights to equal rewards (since they are now both legal and moral imperatives) beyond pointing out that money may currently have even more importance to women than to many men because of its prominence as a measure of worth.

Tokenism still prevails in the employment of women; they are often given visibility in the form of offices, furnishings, and public contact assignments in place of equal pay or opportunity to earn. Hence, women may at present have greater interest in dollars than men.

The more people earn, the more they are satisfied with life

This, too, is a myth. Money is significant and is even overwhelming in its importance to some people, but most of us become aware fairly early in life of its limits in creating happiness. The myth that the more people make the more they are satisfied with life is probably encouraged by the powerfully attractive idea that there is a direct relationship between the amount of pay received and how satisfied the employee is. However, the idea has little substance. People seem to know what pay is appropriate for their work, as the following examples show:

1. A company with heavy turnover, about 40 percent annually, offered a bonus to employees for staying. Nonetheless, turnover increased. Why? Employees felt there was a catch: They could not believe they should be paid extra for doing what they were supposed to do for their base pay. Therefore, when management offered a bonus for doing what was seen as a nonbonus routine aspect of their jobs, employees felt something further was wrong and turnover increased.

2. Young engineers were offered a choice of what starting salary they wanted. At the time the general salary level for engineers starting their careers was $12,000–$15,000. Nobody accepted a job at $10,000; but neither did anyone accept a job at $30,000. The engineers were suspicious of an amount of money they knew was more than they were worth in the open market. In the Sherlock Holmes mystery story called "The Red-Headed League," one of the clues that led the detective to suspect foul play was the disproportion between the amount paid and the services requested.

3. Four executives in a building material supply company were paid about 50 percent more than industry levels. Further, there were too many of them for the amount of work required. The result was that they took no risks; their jobs and their lives were in a rut, and the company was gradually wasting away.

Elliott Jaques, the English management consultant, has suggested that people have a clear idea of the relationship between the recognized value of their jobs (pay) and the length of time a person can operate without his boss's checking on him. Jaques suggests that the president of the company makes decisions that will not be evaluated for a year, the department head for a month, the foreman for a week, and the individual worker on a daily basis. The salary of each should be related to the amount of time his decisions can go without being checked.

The effect of a compensation program depends on how it is introduced as well as on the amounts of money involved

We believe that to be true. An imposed compensation program is less effective than one that participants share in developing. Even when an employer is generous, benevolent, and sensitive to the needs and wishes of his employees, a fringe benefit or incentive compensation program imposed from above will not be as well received or as effective as one which includes contributions from those affected.

In one case in which the authors were professionally involved, they were saved possible embarrassment by getting the early participation of the five departmental managers for whom an incentive program was to be designed. Top management had proposed five individual plans to motivate and to increase corporate profits. Fortunately, each of the managers was asked how he could do a better job and what standards of performance would be fair. Each of the five came back and said that, since their work was so closely interrelated, the effect of creating individual incentives would be to destroy the close business and personal relationship they had developed and cherished.

They therefore suggested that the bonus be based on corporate profits related to salary levels, with a small discretionary amount left for outstanding performance by any one manager. With modest adjustments, a plan such as they suggested was implemented and proved to be effective.

A compensation program based on the cafeteria approach is impractical
That is a myth. The cafeteria style can be used to advantage, and its benefits generally outweigh its problems. In Chapter 7, "Fringe Benefits," we discuss some of the techniques that the small-company manager can apply in adopting the cafeteria style of compensation.

COMPENSATION POLICIES THAT DEMOTIVATE

It may be helpful for managers working on compensation programs to have a group of guidelines that are negative, things to be avoided, which have historically been shown to do almost exactly the opposite of what any compensation program should be aimed to do—change behavior in ways helpful to an organization. Let us look at some demotivating compensation policies, many of which stem from a fear of hurting people or from neglecting to relate performance and rewards.

Giving Equal Raises to All

Ostensibly set up to avoid divisiveness, the policy of giving equal raises to all usually stems from the desire to avoid face-to-face individual appraisals. But the policy produces more ill effects than good ones. Giving equal raises, either in absolute amounts or in percentages, results in a gray organization in which pay has no relationship to performance and in which the few outstanding performers go unrecognized and are turned off. Why should a top performer continue to work (or stay with the company) if he is rewarded no differently from those performing at levels lower than his own?

Putting a Limit on Bonus Pay

An effective way to demotivate people is to put a limit on bonus pay. One company had an incentive bonus arrangement for its five top executives, who together held 20 percent of the stock. The bonus system provided for a maximum of 50 percent of their base pay, and because of their good work in exploiting a growing market, they had earned the full bonus in each of the last four years. The chairman of the board, who owned 60 percent of the stock, wanted to move into a promising new market, entrance to which would have required substantial effort and a reduction in the next two years' profits. The bonus would have been eliminated or reduced.

However, the five executives opposed the move, not on its own merit but because they did not want to risk their bonuses. In addition to the possible loss or reduction of the bonus, the long-term effect of adding the new market to their business portfolio would not have given them one dollar more unless their base salaries were increased. Since the chairman felt that base salaries were more than adequate, the offer to work hard for nothing obviously had to be received with no enthusiasm.

In Chapter 5, we will discuss the question of limits on bonus. In this case, it was clear that the limit was demotivating.

Being Insensitive to Compensation Issues

Never treat a question about compensation lightly. If an issue about pay isn't dealt with in a sincere and dignified fashion, only trouble will result, as the following case illustrates.

A salesman who was being paid a flat salary plus a discretionary bonus asked his president to increase his base salary from the $25,000 level, where it had been stuck for two years. The salesman explained that because of inflation he was having trouble maintaining basic expenses and family (noninsured) medical care. The president answered that business had not been good, and cited as evidence that he had to put up with his 14-month-old Lincoln Continental. He denied the salesman's request for a raise. His crass insensitivity was guaranteed to reduce the salesman's interest in his work, if not for a year, certainly for several months.

Paying Too Much Money to Too Many People

When a compensation program provides people with more money than they deserve, it acts to reduce the total amount of initiative and overall quality of risk taking at that level. When more money is paid than deserved, one of two conditions prevails: Either there are too many good people for the work to be done, or (as is more likely) ordinary performers are being rewarded the same as good ones. In either situation the firm loses.

Example. Three executives were overpaid for their work. They were complacent and saw no reason to improve the company. They were not interested, for example, in taking advantage of an expansion opportunity in a nearby city which was growing faster than their own market. By moving into the market they could have prevented competition from coming in and becoming a threat on the border of their existing market.

The moral of this story: Staff leanly if you want people to work and take risks, and simplify the problems of compensation. In the foregoing case the three executives were psychologically fat, underworked, and overpaid. As a result, they could see no advantage to spending the effort necessary to negotiate, acquire, and integrate the additional plant. Their compensation helped blind them to the nearby potential threat.

Overstaffing is not difficult to detect. It has many obvious symptoms. For example, a simple symptom of overstaffing shows up in companies that have a seasonal cycle. When they do not have to incur overtime during the busy period, they are overstaffed.

Putting the Company Last

A printing manufacturer paid its salesmen, many of whom were stockholders in the company, a flat 5 percent commission on sales.

Because business was obtained through negotiated pricing, a pattern had developed over the years by which the salesmen had the right to set prices and, thereby, the markup.

The results were disastrous for the company. For example, if a salesman was fighting for a $100,000 order, he saw no problem in meeting the potential customer's demand to cut the price $5,000 since the reduction of his commission was only $250 (5 percent of the $5,000 reduction). But the tactic produced a problem for the company: Although the salesman lost only $250 on the transaction, the company lost $4,750 of revenue. Under this policy, in which the company came last and the salesman first, many of the salesmen earned between $100,000 and $200,000 in commissions whereas the company lost between $300,000 and $500,000 for several years.

When a new president was engaged, he immediately changed the commission arrangement so that the salesmen received a percentage of the gross profit. Further, the president centralized price setting and for the first six months took responsibility for reviewing every price cut below bidding standards. The result was that if a $5,000 cut in price was made, the salesman's loss, instead of being only $250, was as much as $1,000.

Mixing Up Ownership and Compensation

A large distributorship was owned equally by five families. Each had one executive in his forties working for the company. Three of the men were average managers; the other two were outstanding. The pay arrangement was simple: Four of the managers received $90,000 a year and the fifth, the nominal president, received $95,000. All received the same benefits.

The result of the equalization of compensation to ownership was that the two good men felt little motivation to work, while the three who were overpaid accepted the money with complacency.

Making Differentiation in Pay Levels Insignificant

In a professional organization only $5,000 (the difference between $80,000 and $75,000) separated the few top performers from those at the next level. The result was a steady turnover of top people who felt that the difference in rewards was not worth the difference in contribution, performance, or responsibility. Since the compensation decisions were made by the whole group (by definition, average), a lid was put on the amount the top people could receive. The restraint eventually brought the bright, ambitious members of the organization to the point of frustration where the only relief was to leave.

Keeping Outdated Pay Differences

Three brothers joined the family business when they emerged from college or army service. Their father set their pay as they entered the business. Twenty years later (ten years after their father had died) the three brothers were still keeping the same pay differential. We could find no relationship between what they were earning and what they were worth.

The problem, once again, was that the outstanding performer (the middle brother) felt that he was locked into a position that had been set twenty years ago and was now totally irrelevant. As so often occurs in many family situations, his resentment over the lack of difference was exacerbated by his wife. She saw the differences in performance, the long hours he put in, the heavier responsibilities he had assumed, and she resented the fact that her sister-in-law and the oldest brother (who received higher pay because he had come into the business two years earlier) were living on a higher scale than they were able to afford. Effective control by the two average performers forced retention of the inherited pay scale.

Saying One Thing, Paying for Another

In an international consulting firm the managing partner worked over a long period to train the staff and build up the firm's professional skills. To emphasize to his partners the importance of training, he added a special section on training activities in the partner evaluation form. When the annual profit was distributed, it became clear that it was not the partner who had devoted time to training who received the big distribution but those who had put in long hours, obtained new clients, and handled large fees. The result was that on-the-job training practically stopped, and the production of dollars became the sole focus of partner effort.

Because pay is the clearest signal of what you want, you create confusion and bitterness and effectively turn off those people who did what you said when you ask for one thing and pay for another.

Putting the Family First

Two sons, their father, and a son-in-law each owned 25 percent of a small midwestern manufacturing company. One son, an attorney, received $15,000 as an inactive director. The other son took the same amount in unsubstantiated travel and entertainment expenses. The father, who was retired, had real estate in Florida, paid his real estate bookkeeper $10,000 out of company funds, and took $5,000 in expenses to visit his properties. The son-in-law, who was running the company, took $15,000 in phony petty cash expenses in order to pay for the interest on the third mortgage required to support his $400,000 home.

Although honest taxpayers were hurt by the $60,000 of improper expenses, among the family the equity was even. Someone might say, "Aside from the tax issue, who was hurt?" The answer is simple: The company was hurt. It is almost impossible in a small company to avoid having other employees know what is going on. In this case the purchasing agent, who was responsible for buying $15 million worth of goods a year, observed: "If the owners don't respect the company's assets, why should I? I have little reason to save the extra half to one percent that might be available through applying extra effort in purchasing when it will only be stolen by the owners."

Don't abuse your assumed ownership rights. If the company's assets are not respected and the time of its owner-executive-managers is not rewarded on the basis of contributions to the firm, employees cannot be expected to respect the company's assets or their use of time.

Using Longevity as the Sole Basis for Promotion

Managers in one company, whose base salaries were $35,000 to $40,000, received raises routinely. Younger, competent workers were frustrated because the company had no appraisal system and they could see no chance to receive promotions or substantial pay increases until the older men were retired. The result was that the good younger workers stayed only long enough to obtain experience; then they left. The deadwood, of course, stayed behind.

The company's priorities had never been thought through or explicitly stated, but it was clear that the compensation system said: "Stay for a long time; raise no questions; cause no problems; and, if you stay healthy, you will move ahead and receive more money." Companies that need bright, creative, risk-taking managers cannot afford a compensation system that pays only for longevity and not for contributions.

Firing People Instead of Giving Them a Chance to Take a Pay Cut

The Peter Principle has become part of basic management literature. Among other things, it states that a person is promoted to the level of his incompetence, from which he cannot be promoted any further. There is another side to the Peter Principle which suggests that incompetence must have existed elsewhere before the person was promoted. The person who made the decision to promote the manager to his level of incompetence is the one responsible for the move as much as the promoted person.

The promotion of a successful salesman to become an incompetent sales manager is a common example. The salesman may be responsible for his own inadequate performance as a sales manager, but it is nearer the truth to say that the person who promoted the salesman exercised poor judgment first.

The point is that mistakes made in promoting people often end in the termination of the incompetent manager. A better alternative in smaller companies is to give the person who has failed but was competent in the past an opportunity to return to his old position or another one suited to his skills with a pay cut appropriate to the new position.

In our experience most executives given a chance to return to a job that they can handle with lower pay will accept the offer *if* they are helped to do so with dignity. This alternative has two benefits: It restores the employee to productive work, and it conserves skills and experience useful to the company. The best way to accomplish a psychologically acceptable demotion is for the manager who made the ill-fated promotion in the first place to accept at least part of the blame and say in effect: "I made a mistake. I took Joe, a superb salesman, and put him into the sales manager's job where his skills could not as well be used. We don't want to lose Joe as a salesman and are therefore asking him to put his sales skills to work for us again."

Because courage is not a common managerial trait, this approach is rarely used. However, when it is used, the assets of skills, knowledge, and experience can be saved and a demotion turned into a positive motivating influence for all who witness it.

This brief listing of inadequate or demotivating evaluation and compensation methods should not lead the reader to believe that we are unaware of the complexities of appraising and assessing performance, which lie at the root of paying for results. Measuring performance is extremely hard to do with complete objectivity *and* justice, especially when it is complicated by family relationships and stock ownership. Performance standards are more often chosen because they ease the appraisal process than because they are equitable.

Small company managers avoid the evaluation problem by relying on current levels of pay and ownership interests. This is comparable to the use of net worth in measuring the value of a closely held company. The IRS, in its regulations describing the different ways a company can be evaluated, lists book value as only one of the techniques. It is commonly used by default since the other measures of an organization's value are much more difficult to use than the simple, bald difference between the company's assets and its liabilities.

By pointing out common compensation problems, we hope you will more easily avoid repeating them in your own plan.

3

Compensation and Motivation

FREQUENTLY, in social and consulting conversations, we hear managers say: "People don't want to work anymore. It makes no difference what we offer, we can't find good people to fill the jobs."

Is the work ethic dead? We doubt it. Even though lifestyles have influenced more than they used to the choice of the type of work and effort a person wants or will allow himself to get involved in, we are among those who still think people want to work, want to give strenuously of themselves, feel it is important that they contribute to their operations, and will accept objective and realistic decisions about what they are worth. They may be skeptical of the place of the company in their lives, but they are still interested in proving themselves, want to grow, and are concerned about the health of the companies they work for as long as the firms are deserving of that concern.

The young breed of managers is enthusiastic and eager to perform. They see themselves as professionals, loyal to their professions or specializations; they rarely expect to stay with dear old Acme Machine or Computer Works all their working lives. From their supervisors they expect high professionalism, rational decisions, help to grow, and honest evaluations. Irving Shapiro, chairman of du Pont, gave advice on dealing with the new breed: "Give them a chance to learn and contribute as individuals, and recognize their contributions. Honor them by keeping them informed about the business, by soliciting their views, and by respecting them from the day they first report to work."*

Devising a compensation program for young tigers is not easy; it must reconcile the older generation's priorities of loyalty and longevity with the practicalities of the limits of any repetitive experience. (Most of us exaggerate the value of our own experience, especially since it was usually unplanned.) Pay must be competitive and offer the chance to earn substantial amounts for hard work and performance. We cannot wait a year to review and reward performance. Good people want fast feedback and, as long as inflation continues, fast changes in their pay, at least semiannually, and in the case of outstanding young managers, quarterly.*

Implicit in any compensation plan are assumptions about human behavior. In this chapter we will consider the powers of compensation to influence behavior and some principles for tightening the connections between pay and contributory behavior. Toward that end, it will be helpful to review some of the well-known theories on behavior in organizations.

A theory or a combination of theories of motivation lies behind every compensation plan. Often the theory or theories are at variance with how we deal with people on other grounds. For example, in directing people most of us deal with subordinates as individuals. We have learned that we have to cajole Charlie, be extremely sensitive to Mary's changing feelings, push Harry, psychologically bribe Jim, and give frequent public recognition to George. We do the same in our family and social relationships, where we have learned what generally works with each individual. Effective compensation programs usually are based on assumptions of human behavior consonant with scientific findings.

Any motivational theory which disregards individual makeup is impractical and factually invalid; no defensible theory can assume that everyone acts the same way for the same reason at the same time. Yet, many privately framed theories do just that. The work of

*Louis Banks, "Here Come the Individualists," *Harvard Magazine*, Sept.–Oct. 1977.
Business Week, September 12, 1977.

making the most efficient use of our limited resources—time, management effort, money, titles, and good jobs—will benefit both from an awareness of the findings of behavioral scientists who have studied people at work and from the ability to relate them to smaller company compensation systems. Otherwise, the compensation planner is indeed limited to generalizing from his random, personal experiences.

THEORIES MOST USEFUL IN THE DEVELOPMENT OF A COMPENSATION SYSTEM

A number of findings of behavioral scientists hold implications for compensation practices and policies in the smaller firm. Here is what a few of them say about how people feel about their work and their companies:

1. Most managers want to respect the company they work for and the person under whom they work. They prefer to be able to talk about their employer's products, services, standards, and image in a way that makes the manager look decent. They want to look up to their superiors as worthy of emulation.

2. Since so much of our self-image comes from our work, people want respect from their boss. Most people need the support of others' opinions to develop feelings about themselves. An employee's positive feelings about himself are supported by respect rather than disdain, by expectations of competence and honesty rather than of failure and lack of trust.

3. People define themselves by their work: what they do, how society measures it, and in part, how society pays for it.

The three generalizations say a lot about compensation policies. A company that pays competitive or better wages implies that its workers are as good as others or better; a boss who has high standards, is impartial, and recognizes performance in distributing promotions and rewards justifies respect from his subordinates; and if compensation rewards a manager's controllable, achievable, individually produced results, he can more easily develop healthy self-respect.

One other generalization, not universally agreed to by behavioral scientists, may add a dose of intellectual humility to any single motivational theory. It is the contingency theory of leadership proposed by Fred Fiedler. Simplified, the theory states that a leader's performance depends on (1) the degree to which the situation gives the leader control and influence, and (2) the leader's basic motivation (whether his self-esteem depends on getting the job done or on having close supportive relations).

The contingency theory suggests that the job- or task-motivated leader performs best where he has either a high degree of control or relatively little control, and the relationship-motivated leader performs best where he has moderate control, requiring tact and individual sensitivity. The theory also tells us that compensation aimed at changing performance will work only when the leader and subordinate relationship is right for *that* situation. The freedom of the individual or the leader to act, the degree of control of results, the level of skill of the subordinates, and the willingness and need of the leader to share information, control, and rewards form a complex matrix which will influence the compensation plan.

The Hawthorne Findings

For the last 20 years several motivational theories have dominated management thinking and affected the type and size of rewards as well as job and organizational design, communications, and information and decision sharing. Earlier, the Hawthorne experiments of 50 years ago demonstrated that changing work conditions were not as significant in changing productivity as were group norms and pressures and the social structure of the groups in which people worked. Some managers have read into the Hawthorne experiments the message that merely paying attention to people will cause them to work more effectively, especially when the managers did not aim at exploitation.

The Hawthorne data have yielded varying interpretations, and that fact should keep us from being dogmatic about motivation theory. As Peter Drucker has said, we write so much about motivation because we know so little about it.

The Linking-Pin Concept

Several behavioral scientists (especially Rensis Likert) have investigated the behavioral effects of the different relationships that can exist between groups and their leaders and have come up with some interesting findings. For example, they found that the influence a manager exercises at the management level above him positively affects his relationships with his subordinates. They also found that the influence a leader permits his subordinates to have over him increases by the same degree his influence over them.

The two findings demonstrate that all enterprises are held together by "pins," each one of which connects two or more groups, and all together form the social organization.

For compensation, the linking-pin concept implies that a manager will be more effective if he can get raises and promotions for his subordinates. It also states that he will be more effective if he listens to his subordinates in setting their standards of performance and pay. "Listens to" does not mean abdicating his financial responsibility, but being sensitive to the needs and feelings of the people whose productivity and compensation he has a great deal to do with.

Theory X and Theory Y

Douglas McGregor in *The Human Side of Enterprise** put forth a theory of motivation that has attracted wide interest and exerted wide influence. Expanded by others, his ideas epitomize the human resources approach to management.

Theory X and Theory Y expressed McGregor's summary points. Vastly oversimplified, Theory X encapsulated a philosophy of life which assumed that people worked only because they had to; that they have to be continually watched, cajoled, threatened, and bribed to get them to do what you want them to. Most people are unwilling to accept responsibility and mainly seek security. Therefore, constant supervision is necessary to accomplish tasks.

Theory Y expressed the opposite philosophy of why people work. This philosophy accepts as fact that people have to work to survive, but also holds that in our society work represents much more than just the means to survival. People work because it is as natural as sleeping and eating; work provides a major source of positive self-image and satisfaction of social needs. The willingness and ability to handle responsibility are more widely dispersed through society than generally recognized, but negative assumptions

*Douglas McGregor, *The Human Side of Enterprise* (New York: McGraw-Hill, 1960).

about people, as exemplified by Theory X, reduce the number of people who are willing to step forward. Theory Y accepts that not everyone is psychologically mature, work is often dull, and some people are unwilling to take risks.

But McGregor pointed out that Theory Y gave the manager more choices, depending on the need at the time and the people he dealt with. And that is the importance of the theories from the compensation viewpoint.

The Drive-for-Achievement Theory

David C. McClelland has spent a professional lifetime investigating the need for achievement. The need for achievement (nAch) is variously determined—by culture, family and personal relationships, life experiences. Whatever the source, the need influences occupational choice and the way people respond to their jobs.

People with high nAch tend to carefully calculate risks and set realistic achievement goals, want to be left alone to solve problems, have a high sense of closure, and want feedback on how well they are doing. Compensation is one of the clearest sources of that feedback. People with low nAch tend to be more concerned with acceptance by others, social activities, relatively unchallenging tasks, and rewards for activity rather than results.

The intrinsic reward (of accomplishing their assumed tasks) motivates people with high nAch, whereas people with low nAch look more for the extrinsic rewards usually represented by lower-level needs. Most entrepreneur-minded managers have high nAch. Their pay should be as much a reward as a scorecard. Follow the rules and give them freedom, help them set goals that tie into the company's, and leave them alone.

From the compensation-planning viewpoint the achievement theory is important because achievers are rare birds who require special handling. An encouraging point is that the need for achievement can be developed through reinforcing experiences.

The Hierarchy-of-Needs Theory

Abraham Maslow proposed that people act to satisfy their needs, which he identified as having five levels:

1. Physiological needs—food, shelter, sex.
2. Security needs—safety at home, security from being fired on the job.
3. Social, belonging needs—being loved in a family, being accepted on the job.
4. Recognition and status needs—growth on the job, peer approval, signs of achievement.
5. Self-actualization needs—using skills, interest, and talents to their maximum.

A major premise of Maslow's system, with significant implications for compensation planning, is that you cannot appeal to someone's higher-level needs until his lower-level needs are first satisfied. Lower-level needs are immediate and therefore constant, and must be satisfied to release energies and effort for the higher needs.

Maslow's theories were widely accepted, in part because they had a humanistic appeal and were understood by many managers. The principle that people are naturally driven to strive for higher-level achievements as their lower-level needs are satisfied was appealing to managers. Because "higher" implies "better," the theory offered a simple guide to the manipulation of environmental factors in the race for employee productivity.

Maslow's views explained the failure or increasing weakening of some of the traditional approaches to behavior control. For example, the threat to fire someone if he fails to perform has been a management tool for generations. However, where competent people are in short supply and they can find positions at will, the tool has declining effectiveness.

Although it has succeeded in explaining the failures of some management approaches to behavior control, Maslow's model of human behavior has its flaws. For example, people do not automatically and routinely move to the fulfillment of higher levels when their lower-level needs are satisfied. Others may move up the scale but get their satisfactions outside their work. Some people do not want promotions or more responsibility; they are concerned only with their security and working conditions. Others become hedonistic and self-centered instead of self-actualized. When they have the time to work at growing, they go fishing or watch TV instead.

The·Hygiene Theory

In a series of studies done with people in different jobs and countries, Frederick Herzberg identified two separate groups of behavior-influencing factors in work—the maintenance and motivating factors. He asked people to describe when they felt good and when they felt bad about their work. Analyzing their answers, he concluded that people felt bad (work turned them off) when the maintenance factors—working conditions, policies and procedures, fringe benefits, basic pay, and supervisory attitudes—were deficient. When they felt good, they listed elements in the work itself—recognition, growth, peer approval (Maslow's influence can be seen).

Herzberg explained to the satisfaction of many that personnel policies such as retirement plans, bowling teams, and background music had little positive influence over work performance. If a company's pay or benefits are substandard, employees will be unhappy (that is, not moved to superior performance). Then, let's say you bring them up to standard, expecting productivity and morale to improve. Morale, as measured by comments about the working environment, may be measurably improved, but it is unlikely that productivity will be improved equally (if it improves at all). According to Herzberg, you have merely removed an irritant, not added a positive factor. Pay can fall between the maintaining and motivating elements: If it is inadequate, it dissatisfies; when brought up to an expected level, it is no longer a dissatisfier, which is not the same thing as being a motivator.

Some critics of Herzberg's findings feel that there is a self-serving aspect to the categories of answers to his questions. The things that make us unhappy at work are in the external world, the company environment over which we have little influence. The things that make us feel good are the things we control, and they lie largely within. Is it possible that we place the responsibility in the work environment for the things that make us feel bad and want to take credit for the things that make us feel good?

Whatever the answer, in our opinion Herzberg has much to offer managers in smaller companies. Other studies have shown that people at many organizational levels are primarily concerned with the maintenance aspects of their jobs. Until they are freed from that concern, you can't expect much commitment, initiative, or risk taking. Even the acceptance of rational change, that is, needed or beneficial, nondisruptive change, seems to be related to the acceptance by staff of the adequacy of their maintenance factors.

The Reinforcement Theory

B. F. Skinner, whose work led to the recent surge of interest in behavior modification, wrote that we can study behavior but we cannot learn much (nor should we spend the time trying) about people's motives. Motives are hidden deep within us; they are usually unknown even to the holder and extraordinarily hard for outsiders to identify and fathom. We should be concerned with observing how people behave in response to the signals the organization sends out, assessing the value of the responses to the firm, and then trying to modify the behavior so as to make it more congruent with the firm's objectives by changing the signals and/or the rewards.

Skinner's main contribution, from the compensation viewpoint, may be that he gave us insight into the value of fast feedback (which includes rewards). When someone does what we want him to do, Skinner tells us we should reinforce that behavior (increase the inclination to behave that way again) by rewarding it. When someone performs in a way we do not want, we can "punish" the behavior (weaken the incentive to behave that way again) by withholding rewards.

Consider the implications of this theory for reward systems in smaller companies. It implies that when someone does what we want and we want that behavior to continue, we must reward him in a way that is meaningful to *him*—and quickly. From that point of view the annual performance and salary reviews practices in most companies are inadequate. During such reviews the performance that took place over the preceding year is lumped together in a single evaluation (or at best a series of evaluations) and then rewarded in the form of a raise or a bonus. The connection between *specific* behavior and reward is lost.

From answers to the question we have put to hundreds of respondents—"Why did you get the specific raise or bonus that you received at your last review session?"—we know that very few managers in smaller companies know why they got what they did in the form of extra compensation, and they cannot say (the other side of the same coin) what they have to do to earn more.

Skinner's suggestion that fast feedback be given when desired performance takes place should not be taken to mean that a raise or bonus should be awarded every time someone performs *well,* particularly at the managerial level where such performance is expected. It does mean, however, that *exceptional* performance should be sought out, lauded, and rewarded at strategic points, and those points should not be widely spaced.

Note the implications for flexibility in compensation planning this point contains. Although standard performance for many jobs amounts to good, acceptable, or average (whatever that means) performance and normally is not rewarded, rewards can be given for such performance when it is exceptional for the performer. In short, rewards can be used to *alter* behavioral patterns as well as sustain them.

The feedback (recognition and reward) need not be paced by formal performance systems or the timing of reviews. If you wish to encourage and reinforce the behavior that produces the results you want, you must take notice early, provide feedback quickly, and reward appropriately.

Because taste, imagination, and individual needs enter the picture, cash need not be the only form of reward given. Money is always worth considering, but sincere thanks, time off, public recognition, being asked to sit in on a problem-solving session, even being given a special task (with potential for further reward), a gift of two tickets to a sporting event—these are only a few examples of the many kinds of rewards available to the sensitive manager. Determine what you want, watch for it, reward it.

The Skinner principles put to work to modify behavior may be an unacceptable form of manipulation or smack of animal training to some. But that concern, in view of the difficulty of managing an enterprise to the benefit of consumers, employees, and stockholders, is unjustified. Behavior modification used to produce such benefits is not immoral. Among other things, it is not a self-sustaining process. As Herzberg has shown, the effects of manipulation are not long-lasting (a reward loses value in proportion to the number of times it is given). Furthermore, people cannot always be "bought"; they have an immense ability to do what they think is right for *them.* All of us act in our own interests much of the time; we rarely work against what we think is right for ourselves.

The most ingenious user of rewards to modify behavior can practice his art comfortably knowing that we cannot get people in a free society to do what they do not want (and their independence is steadily increasing). We can increase the probability that they will do what *we* want if we offer rewards, appropriate to them and the occasion and fast and direct enough so that they can see the connection.

The Expectancy Theory

Developed by Victor Vroom and Edward Lawler III, among others, the expectancy theory offers a framework for compensation so basic that we have never seen a plan work which violated its tenets. The tenets themselves are simple, but for them to work they must all be present in the pay plan and interconnected.

According to this theory, rewards (in the broadest sense) may affect performance when: (1) the reward is considered worth the effort in the mind of the individual (not only his supervisor's), (2) the performance desired is achievable and controllable and not attainable simply by chance or because of external factors, and (3) the individual's efforts are likely to affect the performance.

The following example highlights the first point. What are the odds that a $4,000 bonus for specific performance will affect the effort of a 21-year-old whose base salary is $20,000? With that sketchy information most people would say, "Fairly good." What are the chances that a $4,000 bonus would affect the performance of a 50-year-old whose base salary is $50,000? Most people would say, "Less likely." Applied to a large population of 21- and 50-year-olds, the answers are probably accurate. But if the wife of the 21-year-old has a $50,000 annual trust income, and the 50-year-old is supporting two ex-wives, three children in college, a sick mother, and a greedy 25-year-old girlfriend, the answers will probably change. The example shows that to use compensation effectively you need to know your people and fit the rewards to them as individuals.

For the owner-managers of smaller companies the compensation message from the expectancy theory is: Don't pay people on the basis of your own feelings of what is important. The business means more to you than anyone; you are probably willing to put in long hours, give up personal pleasures, and reduce your family priorities to an extent that no one else in the company is willing to match. You may also have grown up in family circumstances or during a period like the Depression in which money had a different significance from what it may have for some younger people today. Thus, *you* may expect that with overtime, double time, or a special bonus people should be willing to do what you want.

But to them, the extra pay and the pressure, or the giving up of a personal or family routine or event, may just not be worth the reward. Industrial history is full of cases of people who will not work for substantially more money because of the time, hours, risk, or social opprobrium attached.

The other two points from the expectancy theory are basic to compensation programs: (1) make sure that the performance you want is achievable, controllable, and subject to the effort of the individual, and (2) don't give incentives starting at some impossible point or for reasons that have nothing to do with the individual.

Almost any business that dealt with the public made money in Montreal during July 1976 when the Olympics were taking place. In such businesses an incentive plan calling for payment of a bonus on the increase of sales or profits over 1975 would have been neither motivating nor fair to some employees and the stockholders.

The expectancy theory explains some of the limitations of bonuses which are purely discretionary. Since the recipient of a discretionary bonus has no control over the amount or over the reason he receives a bonus, he loses some control over his work.

Related to the expectancy theory is the law of effect: People are likely to produce more when they believe you expect more from them. As Shaw wrote in *Pygmalion,* "The difference between a lady and a flower girl is not how she behaves but how she is treated."

Where the organization of work implies low-level performance and the need for constant supervision, when people are not given the feedback they want, and when the payments made for achievement are small (implying to those who receive payments that the results were not very important), that company can only have a compensation program that says to its people: You are not very capable, you are not worthy of trust, you did not produce the results by yourself, and we are paying you as an inconsequential part of the corporate team.

The Human Resources Management Approach

The human resources approach to management has become so pervasive that only a rash or outraged critic has felt comfortable opposing it. Because most management thinking is now under the influence of the theories of human resources management, most compensation programs derive in some respects from them. The goodness of human beings and their inherent wishes to do better are attractive tenets; to oppose them is unpleasant and disappointing.

However, the realities of organizational life conflict with some of the assumptions of the human resources approach.* Here are a few of the conflicting realities:

Intrinsic aspects of work (Herzberg's motivators) are only one reason people select jobs and why they work in them. Pay, convenience to home, friends, security, physical demands, type of supervision—all of these may be stronger reasons for people choosing and staying in a job than recognition, challenge, professional or technical growth. When asked whether their job is "satisfactory" or what elements they would like changed, few people answer, "Make my work less boring." People seem to find their own level of work satisfaction.

The ideal work and compensation program is one in which the personal goals of the individual can be made compatible with those of the organization. Unfortunately, as has been learned in MBO programs, such compatibility is not often achievable. When it comes to a contest of whose goals to serve, those of individuals must usually be subordinated to those of the firm. Not even in our society can the individual's time, interests, or values be allowed to stand in the way of efficiency. The trick is to avoid the opposition in the first place. That is not always possible.

Two other assumptions that often fail the test of organizational life are that trust and openness enhance organizational success, and that sharing in decisions not only gets employees more involved but produces decisions of better quality. Both assumptions are questionable: Secrecy serves those who control information, and it is hard for many managers who are now making decisions to see how they are helped by giving up the sweet taste of power. Further, as some psychologists have pointed out, when a manager makes decisions which affect his subordinates, he may come to believe that they are inferior to him. He therefore downgrades their ability and justifies his retaining the decisions for himself.

---

*Walter R. Nord and Douglas E. Durand, "What's Wrong with the Human Resources Approach to Management?" *Organizational Dynamics,* Winter 1978.

Power in small, closely held companies is as often tied to ownership as it is to competence. Decisions are not necessarily made for the sake of the company, but because they serve the whims or selfish interest of those with stock ownership. In a context of power retention, secrecy, and privilege, it is hard to relate compensation to controllable performance. Further, to repeat a point that was made earlier, a compensation plan that has not been checked with those affected is less likely to be effective.

Finally, money still counts. Many people look to their families and to social, religious, fraternal, or athletic activities for the satisfactions that the human resource theories imply can be provided by work. From their work they want money, security, some social activity, and the absence of unpleasantness. Therefore, in planning compensation programs, pay attention to Herzberg: Make sure the maintenance parts of the job are satisfactory, pay competitively, and don't expect the work to take all the interests and commitments of your employees.

INTERESTS AND OTHER INTANGIBLES OF MOTIVATION

The real key to motivation lies in giving people the opportunity to satisfy *their* higher needs. The degree to which the opportunity is given is a competitive factor; satisfaction of higher needs always involves higher capacities and that, in turn, always benefits the company, however individualized the employment of the capacities may be. On that score, CEO's do very well; they have more opportunities to satisfy their higher needs than any other employee. The intrinsic rewards of being able to exercise one's talents are among the intangibles of executive compensation. It takes effort and ingenuity to find out how to satisfy higher-level needs at lower organizational levels.

Group Roles and Compensation

Many smaller companies function through groups, the most common ones being the groups of key people, groups of those who cause things to happen. The Industrial Training Research Unit in England examined groups to find out what helped them perform and concluded that groups do two things: (1) they solve problems, prepare schedules, train, perform a task; and (2) they operate through interpersonal relationships which require each member to play a specific role—the task cannot be done well unless the interpersonal skills are adequate. The roles which the ITRU identified are coordinator, idea man, critic, implementer, team builder, external contact, and inspector. The functions of the roles are clear from the titles.

Most individuals can handle two or three roles in the same group. For a group to function at the highest level of effectiveness, it must have a proper balance of all seven roles, usually requiring five to twelve people. In most cases, the group members are competent to evaluate who can fill which role and which role is being weakly performed or is missing.

The significance of this research for compensation in a smaller firm is that you may have to reassess your definition of a key person. Since so much work is done through groups, it may be that the key person is less an individual operator than a good role player. And you may find the quieter, less dramatic roles important enough that you want to pay a premium to attract or retain people who have special skills in playing the less prominent and, therefore, less prized roles.

Example. A trade association used the services of a consultant whose genius lay in his ability to handle the coordinator and team-builder roles. Although he had become knowledgeable about the industry, he was not an idea man, served only temporary roles, and could not implement or perform any of the continuing functions. Good things happened when he was part of the group that did not take place when he was absent: Decisions were made with less unpleasant conflict, more ideas were suggested, better understanding of the place of each member took place, and everyone felt better when he was present. What would the services of such a person be worth within an organization?

Work Satisfaction and Attitude Surveys

Because their positions are inherently more challenging and diversified than those of lower-level people, managers often project their feelings about work to their subordinates. Therefore, attitude surveys are sometimes illusory. Asked the question, "All in all, how well satisfied are you with your job?" about 85 percent of all respondents will give a positive answer. Compare your answer to the doctor's question, "Overall, how well do you feel?" You will probably answer, "Pretty well," or "Better." Meanwhile, you may have a twinge of arthritis, occasional headaches or insomnia, heartburn after overindulgence, and feel guilty about being 15 pounds overweight and smoking 2 packs of cigarettes a day. It is not until the doctor delves into the details of your health that he finds out what lies behind "Pretty well."

Similarly, when feelings about work are probed, about twice as many complaints about the maintenance factors surface as about the motivating ones. That, again, may result from the relationship between individual satisfaction and job level. Because the negatives about job conditions are often correctable or explicable, when you suspect they exist, give people a chance to talk, and listen.*

PAY LEVELS AND JOB DIFFERENCES

People probably get more upset about discrepancies in pay than almost any other personnel matter. They look for internal equity, that is, for job pay differences which are based on differences in educational requirements, experience, pressures endured, amount of supervision of others or over the job itself, unpleasant conditions, and so on. The pay levels often do not match the job differences. One company sought to close the discrepancies by giving the rank and file a free hand to adjust all salaries. Salary costs overall rose by only about 6 percent, but dramatically large changes in salary distribution took place. Despite the changes, which reduced some salaries while raising others, higher job satisfaction and productivity resulted.

The smaller company manager who does not wish to go so far can accomplish similar results by asking in annual (or more frequent) listening sessions with his staff or through surveys: Are the right people getting raises and promotions for the right reasons? Everyone wants more, but almost everyone knows that there are external, competitive limits and internal limits based on the ability to pay and equity in pay relationships. It is extremely disturbing for an em-

---

*For example, it is almost unforgivable in a small company that wants to resist unionization to permit it to take place when it could have been prevented by firm, fair, sensitive treatment of routine personnel procedures, by competitive salaries and benefits, and sensitive listening and action to detect and stop serious complaints before they become cancerous.

ployee to learn that another person working at a significantly lower level of performance or job is receiving the same pay.

The answer is basic: Separate performance and pay significantly. Don't be limited to a salary differential of 10 percent between the top- and bottom-level performers—this may help you keep the lower-level people around (if you want them), but almost guarantees you will turn off the top group early in the game and, ultimately, lose them altogether.

Occasionally, in a fit of frustration a manager will offer a special reward to low performers to get them to move up to ordinary levels. This practice violates the general Skinnerian finding that we should reward the results we want and punish those we don't. What positive effect can there be among the already high-level performers when they see inadequate performance rewarded? Perhaps there is room for a carefully worked out incentive program that rewards significant improvement as long as it keeps a healthy spread between achieved performance levels. It has a higher and safer payoff than training.

SELECTION

Motivational tools will not be effective if a person is in a job for which he is unsuited. Someone without the skills and interests required by the job cannot be directed through organizational pressures or rewards to do what he cannot or will not do. Probably more effort is wasted in trying to get people to do things for which they are unfit than any other output of personnel energy. Selection— fitting the person to the job—is the first and most important step in motivation.

Because the literature relating to the selection process is rich, we will touch on only two aspects of selection which are rarely well considered in smaller companies. Observing the following caveats, along with professional attention to the other basics of selection, may increase your selection success rate to 60–70 percent.

Present the Job Honestly

Don't oversell the job. In your eagerness to attract the rare special person, you may be tempted to color the opportunities and the speed with which the new manager will take over a position or achieve a salary level. If there is a serious distortion between the preview and early experience, you stand the risk of quickly losing or embittering the new employee.

Define the Job's Intangible Qualities

Failure in most managerial jobs, especially in many smaller firms, comes less from technical inadequacy and more from inability to handle certain situations because the job was never carefully defined. Following are several questions to help you arrive at a definition.

1. What is the job's level of ambiguity and uncertainty? Managerial jobs, unlike most functional positions, do not end; they are not characterized by a high incidence of closure; they are better described as processes. When are customers satisfied, employees properly trained, morale so good you can forget it, vendor relations working entirely in your favor, the outside world stable? The answer is never! How significant are these processes to the job, and how long did the applicant operate in a previous ambiguous environment?

2. What is the level of personal relationships—does the job require pleasantness, sufficient charm or attractiveness so that people are not turned away, or does it require long relationships in which care and concern for a few people matter? The flight attendant, salesman, receptionist, dining-room hostess, and others who deal with many people are in the first group. Managers and others who usually work with the same people fall in the second group. They have to feel comfortable knowing that they cannot run away from unpleasant personal relationships.

3. Does the job require problem solving or problem prevention? Managerial jobs usually require problem solving; highest-level positions are best filled by people who boast less of the number of problems they handled and more of those they prevented from arising. Problem solvers are visible; they cause dramatic results because they eliminate something everybody sees. Problem preventers work quietly; they create normally dull organizations in which most crises have been anticipated and only the occasional unanticipated event or planned change disrupts routine.

4. Does the job involve skill in following the rules or in taking initiative where there are no rules?

These questions, thoughtfully considered, can help you define the key elements in a job. They point out the limits of trying to change behavior through compensation. Most organizations need people with all the skills mentioned—problem solvers and problem preventers are a typical example.

Emphasize the Advantages of Working for the Small Company

If your sales are under $50 million, you may feel that in selecting personnel you have to take the leavings of large firms who offer glamor, security, potential, power, and large pay. In an earlier book* we commented on techniques small companies can use to attract good people and the advantages of working for the small company that should permit it to get the few first-rate people it needs and can financially and organizationally support. True, differentials between starting salaries offered by large and small firms are significant; smaller firms usually cannot offer more than 75 percent of the going rate for top graduates of the top business schools without destroying their salary scale. Nevertheless, they can succeed in going after and catching first-rate people.

Competence shows and is respected in all organizations, especially in the smaller ones where it is difficult for one to hide or be hidden. If you hire a young bright manager and he proves himself quickly (provided you give him the chance), there will be few objections to his receiving dramatic raises and bonuses. We therefore suggest: Hire the top people you need (the organization can tolerate only a few), bring them in at salaries as high as your present scale allows, and promise frequent specific raises and bonuses for specific performance. The advantages of working for the small company often overcome the discrepancy in starting salaries.

Example. A very small ($800,000 annual volume) client of ours was experiencing the disorders and pains of rapid growth and was convinced by us to hire a marketing manager. Their first objections were quickly dealt with but their last took a long time to answer: "We can't afford a person with skills at that level." In time, the client agreed to try to hire one, and the search turned up a candidate with almost ideal qualifications who had worked for two large companies. He responded to the advertisement of a small firm, he said, because he was tired of commuting and the big-firm "rat race." When offered the job, he demanded a salary almost equal to his current earnings (the ad had not specified a salary range), which was out of the question at the time, as it exceeded the salaries of each of the two

---

Survival & Growth: Management Strategies for the Small Firm (New York: AMACOM, 1974).

owners of the business. Finally, one of the negotiators said, "Look, join us at a salary our present compensation pattern can stand and accept our word there'll be a lot more in the future. We can't even tell you how much more because we haven't developed a plan yet, but take our word for it, there'll be more." As open-ended and unsupported as the offer was, the candidate accepted the job at two-thirds of his current earnings. Not long after, his shifting around of product lines and adapting products to new markets multiplied sales several times over, and his compensation almost trebled during his six-year tenure.

Before he left, amicably and to start his own business, he said to the owners of the business, which had grown to $5 million, "The main reason I joined you at a lower salary than I was making was your confidence in your company's future and the trust you generated in me that you'd share the benefits of growth. Oh, and there was one more thing; you made me feel you needed *me* and would give me all the room I would need to really do a job for you."

The case points up the attractiveness of compensation elements other than cash. We have kept contact with the departed marketing manager and know that his having helped put his previous employer "on the map" is more a source of satisfaction to him than the money he made, which, in total, exceeded what he was likely to have made if he had stayed in his last large company job.

ELEMENTS OF WORK THAT DIRECT BEHAVIOR

In smaller firms the influence of top people can be felt more directly, because the style and atmosphere of management do not have to filter through many levels. Therefore, if they follow some basic work philosophy rules, smaller companies can raise the chances of keeping people and directing their behavior.

Make All Work Decent

The cheapest compensation element available to a company is the dignity, the importance and recognition, it confers upon jobs. In particular, the jobs that need to be dignified are jobs which do not produce visible results or, if visible, do not have an impact on the bottom line, that demand low levels of skill, or offer low levels of stimulation or variation. Managerial and staff jobs below the top may suffer from a lack of visibility and challenge. When the jobs are considered dignified, decency and worth are imparted to those who do the jobs.

Provide the Maximum Reasonable Job Security

We know that people are loyal first to themselves, then to their peers and co-workers, and finally to their company. Cutting labor costs ultimately means firing people. To almost every employee it is clear that his interest in job security and the company's interest in making more profits are in conflict. To free the knowledge about the job that lies within almost every person, you have to convince him that he and his friends will not suffer when he introduces cost-cutting improvements. Labor savings cannot be allowed to end in suicide or fratricide.

Smaller companies that have developed a sense of stability, belonging, and a consultative or participative management style have done so because they have flatly promised their workers (from managers down) that no one will lose his job because of the introduction of labor-saving methods. In such companies the conviction exists that the savings will be realized only through attrition or the absorption of higher volumes by the present workforce.

The advantages of this technique in the closely held company are, first, that if trust has been built up through past personnel policies, the statement will be accepted and savings can be made quickly; second, the savings can be accelerated if they are shared with the staff (an old idea, but one which makes incentive a companywide affair). Lincoln Electric Company's cost-saving, profit-sharing plan remains a long-time successful example.

Be Consistent

No single motivational or compensation technique will work in isolation, and no compensation plan can ever be designed that rests on one principle alone. Because each compensation plan is complex, founded on and incorporating many diverse elements, the elements should be consistent with each other, should fit together and reinforce each other and the total. Compensation must dovetail with corporate strategy, with ethical values, with the company's willingness to share profits, information, and decisions, with management's expectations about why people work and what kinds of results are compensable, and with all the technical principles upon which the compensation plan is based directly and indirectly.

When the signals are not only clear but consistent, when motivational assumptions are based on behavioral findings as well as individual belief evidenced by daily management decisions, and the structure of rewards fits people, performance, and jobs together, you have a rare organization, one almost impossible to surpass.

Redirect Effort

In periods of flat sales, in a recession, or when corporate strategy dictates goals other than sales growth or other forms of expansion, the compensation system should be adjusted to keep rewards in tune with the changed objectives. Rewards for protection of existing assets (such as customers), for better use of financial assets (higher turnovers), and for cost cutting may be appropriate. The measurements may be negative ("loss of customers not to exceed . . ."), but they are likely to produce the required behavior if they fulfill the standards previously described—controllable, achievable results, with rewards considered worthwhile to the recipient.

MOTIVATION AND THE COMPENSATION PROGRAM

In this section we will describe how the findings of several key motivation studies bear on compensation planning.

Set Individual Pay

Smaller companies have an almost infinite choice of plans they can fit to the individual needs of their managers. Unlike the situation in large companies, where pay equity is usually related to the size of the division or grade level, smaller companies have one person, or a few at the most, at the same level of responsibility and therefore often find salary grade systems inappropriate.

The problem in setting individual pay is that you have to be able to hold individuals accountable for results and be able to identify and measure individual performance. Nevertheless, you should set pay individually whenever you can. The competent, achieving manager will work harder and more creatively if he knows that his pay is realistically connected to what he alone produces.

Avoid situations in which one manager can earn more money only at the expense of another. If you cannot assign individual accountability and responsibility, you may be forced to use group pay, which we will discuss in Chapter 5.

Keep the Basis of Compensation Simple

Most of us can properly attend to only a few things simultaneously. Some psychologists have stated that the maximum number of items anyone can handle is six or seven. Fortunately, few jobs have more than this number of key result areas. A two-page job description listing 20 to 40 tasks for which the manager is responsible probably lies unused for this reason.

In your compensation system concentrate on the few main results wanted, on the outputs not the inputs. You are not paying for hours or sweat as much as you are for results.

Example. A small bank holding company had developed a complicated incentive pay system. In August the president of the company decided to fire the head of one of the small savings and loan subsidiaries. The employment contract with the savings and loan officer called for him to receive a proportion of his annual incentive bonus within 30 days of his termination. The computation was so complicated that he could not be fired until after the end of the year, when the auditors, the only ones able to complete the computation, came in.

Make Large Pay Changes If You Want to Change Performance

In his book *Management by Motivation,** Saul Gellerman stated that a bonus or raise of 20 percent was usually required to make a manager put out the effort necessary for a dramatic change in his performance. A superior does not give a raise; the manager earns it and deserves it. Most managers expect a 10 to 12 percent raise for adequate or better than adequate performance.

Another measure of how much it takes to change a manager's level of effort is that the amount given must be enough so that he can change his standard of living. That does not mean that he can move from a Chevrolet to a Rolls Royce or from a two-bedroom house to a mansion. It does mean that his raise or bonus enables him to have a second car, take at two-week vacation in Europe instead of at the local motel, afford orthodontia for his child, and feel comfortable taking the family out for dinner once a week.

*New York: American Management Association, 1968.

Even if inflation is excluded from this computation, we can see why most good managers do not go down on their knees to thank their bosses when they receive a 10 percent raise. It is not enough to support a significant rise in living standards or justify a change in effort. Star performers look for a raise of 15 to 20 percent perhaps several times a year.

Keep the Performance Standards and the Reward System Stable

One aspect of the expectancy theory, oversimplified, tells us that if your offer of a reward for a certain performance is considered dependable, you increase the odds that the person will work in the direction you want.

A reward system must send out consistent signals, consistent not only for a period of at least a year but consonant with other parts of the management process. The reason for consistency is simple: It promotes expectation that achievement will be rewarded when and how promised.

EMPLOYEES' ACCEPTANCE OF THE SYSTEM

When we deal with pay structure and how job and pay differences are administered, several factors seem to affect employees' evaluation of their job and satisfaction with pay. The chief ones are: (1) the degree to which the pay system is designed for the company and not an ill-fitting adaptation of another company's, and (2) employees' acceptance of the standards used in the evaluation of their performance.

Pay as One of Several Factors

One of the purposes of an effective pay system is reducing the turnover of employees whom management wants to keep. However, the limited evidence available indicates that dissatisfaction with pay is a minor influence in an employee's decision to stay or leave. Pay is only one factor in job satisfaction, and dissatisfaction with pay is often offset by equally powerful positive job influences such as the company's prospects, the holding of power, friends, travel convenience, and so forth.

Leaving a company is only one way of showing unhappiness with pay. Others are working with less interest, spending less time on the job, or making fewer risk-taking decisions.

That money is a major but by no means the only motivator is exemplified by the athlete who is injured and in pain but says nothing and plays out the game until it is finished. He is not motivated by pay but by a sense of being needed, of not wanting to let down his teammates, of not wanting to appear inadequate. Similarly, telephone companies have found that morale was highest among linemen when they were called out to repair lines during a hurricane or tornado. The men might work for more than 36 hours under unpleasant and dangerous conditions, yet their morale was high, not because of their extra pay but because of their sense of being needed, of the worth of their accomplishments, of the testing of their competence.

People in other industries often respond in the same way when called upon for extraordinary effort. They, too, are often exhilarated as much by the pressure and the sense of being needed as by the possibility of additional income.

Money is terribly important under three conditions:

1. When it is the difference between merely surviving and living decently.
2. When it separates a good person from ordinary performers.
3. When it helps keep together people who want to be together.

The three conditions are mentioned primarily to underline a key point: Few of those who, by their own standards, have enough money work primarily for money. Those who work almost exclusively for money are either not receiving as much as they deserve or are in the grip of needs no amount of money can satisfy. The lesson: *Know your key people as individuals and provide enough different satisfactions (money included) for different needs.*

4

Laying the Groundwork for the Plan

THIS chapter deals with the steps to be taken before meaningful, corporate-serving compensation planning can begin. This is the most intensive information-gathering phase in the planning process.

THE STARTING PLACE—SETTING COMPANY GOALS

Compensation planning is not an isolated technique. It is not merely an administrative necessity forced on a company to keep people from quitting for better pay or to join competitors for any reason, and it is always an expression of economic and cultural values. In the most successful smaller companies, compensation planning is recognized as a resource for efficiently realizing their goals and objectives.

Effective compensation planning begins with the setting of high-quality company goals and objectives. When a compensation plan is directed toward reaching corporate goals and supports the firm's strategies, it becomes itself a clearly defined strategy of accomplishment. But for a compensation plan to be so directed, the corporate goals and objectives must first exist.

Existence of goals is not enough, of course. The goals and objectives must also be practical and worthy, that is, capable of being translated into the work to be done, the performance levels to be achieved, and the standards against which performance is to be measured. Undeniably, it is difficult to set acceptable, practical, worthy goals and objectives. But the task must be done if a practical *and* motivating compensation plan is to be made possible.

Key people, particularly, need to have respect for corporate targets and to know what their roles are in reaching the objectives, how they are doing, and the criteria by which they will be paid. To the extent that they know and the pay program ties the elements together, the program will represent a good investment.

Clarity of Corporate Goals

In a closely held company the motives of individual managers and the corporate goals and ownership plans of the majority shareholders may conflict in respect to the rewards for efforts and time frames of accomplishment. Key managers frequently are reluctant to commit themselves to or take risks on new projects with payoffs several years away when they do not know the business aims of the owners. Managers we have known in that position have put it this way: "Will the company still be owned by the same people in three years after this program starts, or will somebody else own it? If the latter, how do I know whether or not the new owners will appreciate what I've done?"

Questions about priorities in decision making and action and where discretionary time should be spent also follow from a lack of direction about corporate purposes: "Are the company owners interested in short-term profits or long-term results? If we don't know, how can we know where best to spend our time to satisfy the owners and earn the highest pay?"

Example. A $30-million-a-year manufacturer had 1,000 outside stockholders who held about 40 percent of the shares. The controlling interest was owned by three officers. The goals were clear but probably off target: Earn 25 percent more each year; increase sales by the same percentage. The goals were questioned by outside members of the board who felt they limited the long-range benefits of market and customer development and focused operating managers' efforts on one year's results.

The compensation system encouraged product managers to propose only projects with a fast one-year payback, which definitely was not in the long-range interests of the firm. When the incentives and rewards came from hitting the annual 25 percent targets, why risk this year's results and bonuses by working at something which might not show a benefit for several years?

ANALYZING THE BUSINESS

Few smaller companies understand clearly and precisely where they can be and where they want to be in two, three, or however many years. When they do express their intentions concerning the future, they usually do so in historical, excessively humble, or vague terms. In most smaller companies someone has to sort objectives out before meaningful work on the compensation plan can begin.

Where the desired future of the firm is not clearly and realistically seen, the process of making it so can be speeded up and materially assisted by formalizing the process. The situation-analysis phase of formal planning is an example of how the process can be formalized.

For clients who do not have an ongoing planning activity, we employ a fact-finding technique that condenses the work of analyzing the elements of a business and establishing a basis for compensation planning. We call the technique "Management Physical®."

The Management Physical®

A Management Physical® is an intensive, short, nondisruptive analysis of the principal aspects of a firm's organization as an operating entity. Over two dozen physicals have identified corporate strengths and weaknesses and yielded possibilities for using compensation better.

We have found that by asking six groups of questions, we can quickly identify and define the major result areas in a company and how well the main functions work together in achieving the results desired. The information yielded also can be used to construct an "economic model" of the company. The phrase will not be acceptable either to econometricians or to management scientists since the questions are substantially nonquantitative and yield little hard data. The answers, however, do provide an incisive description of what the company does, why it exists, what resources it employs, how its key functions relate *(including its reward system),* and what opportunities exist for improving the firm's performance.

In the Management Physical® we first try to identify the unique qualities of a company, its competitive advantages, the product or service benefits it offers its customers; then we see how its major functions relate to the continuance and, possibly, enhancement of its unique qualities and advantages. The information is gathered through interviews with all key people, distribution and analysis of attitude survey forms, meetings with selected groups of employees for open discussion, and examination of plans, policies, personnel manuals, financial statements, evaluation systems, and compensation programs.

The questions we ask in the Management Physical® interviews follow.

Question 1

What do we do uniquely? What is our competitive advantage? Why do people buy from us? Why do people who might buy from us not buy from us? What do our customers think about us? How do our employees, our vendors, and our competitors see us? What do we do well? What have we done poorly in the past?

These questions are aimed at identifying, protecting, and exploiting the company's competitive advantages. The following case illustrates the usefulness of the questions: The top five managers of an equipment distribution company that had been in business for 75 years were asked why its customers did business with it. After much talk and thinking they could not say why customers did business with them other than because of habit—most of their customers were old customers whose "loyalty," apparently, was almost entirely based on habit and familiar associations.

Concerned about the vulnerability brought out by the questions, top management of the company engaged a local market research organization at modest cost to find out why people bought from whom they did and not from others. Among other things, they found that customers were not nearly as interested in equipment advantages as they were in equipment service. They were concerned with the availability and use of equipment rather than ownership, leasing, or minor technical differences between competing brands.

Armed with this information, the president reorganized his company, took advertisements in local newspapers and trade magazines emphasizing the company's service priority, and changed not only the organization, the jobs, and the recognition of who within the company were "key," but the reward system as well.

It is not always easy to identify the unique aspect of a company; the uniqueness is rarely on the balance sheet or otherwise obvious. In a seminar run by one of the authors for a group of supermarket operators, the following were cited as the unique aspects of particular stores:

1. Variety and quality of produce were superior to that offered by other supermarkets.

2. The owners of a four-store chain left merchandising and pricing decisions entirely to the discretion of the local managers, who were able to respond quickly to changing competitive situations.

3. The market offered the only check-cashing facility in the town.

4. Really low prices, no frills, bare-bones merchandising, and short hours differentiated one market.

5. A young manager took over a chain of eight stores as it was approaching bankruptcy and turned it into a unique profit-sharing venture. Because of the variety of locations and situations, he realized that he would not be able to deal uniformly with the problems in each store. He therefore created a nine-man management team in which he and the eight managers had an equal vote. He then divided the profits of the company, which the group was able to produce, on an equal basis.

6. A 450-person, 120,000-square-foot supermarket run by a man in his early sixties was distinguished by his personnel policies. He interviewed every new employee, and at the end of 30 days he, the supervisor, and the new employee reviewed progress and retention. Annually, he listened to every one of his 450 employees. Doing that took fully 50 percent of his time. When asked how he could afford to spend so much time on personnel, he answered, "How can I afford not to?" Other people were capable of such routine work as checking

on prices (they could not be below cost nor substantially more than competition), cleanliness, and advertising. But he believed that the way his people felt about their jobs and the way they treated customers bore critically on making and keeping his market different from the stores of the giant chains around him, and that the only way his employees would know how important they were to the company would be for him to show by his effort and his time how important they were to him.

To summarize the point, the normal curve of distribution applies to companies as it does to most large populations. Most businesses are mediocre, about 10 percent are marginal or going out of business, and 10 percent are superior, in some manner unique. And that is their competitive advantage.

If a compensation system is to be used to a firm's advantage, it must focus on setting the company apart. In other words, if you don't know specifically what performance is needed to serve potential and existing customers in some special way, you cannot use pay to get employees to do the special things that are required to attract and retain customers with greater facility, at lower cost, and/or with greater profit than competitors.

Question 2

What key decisions must we make in order to support our competitive advantage?

Among the questions in this group that reveal whether your decision making is consistent and responsive to the outside world rather than to the owners' selfish motives are the following:

What are the personal goals of the owners? Do they permit sharing of information, decisions, plans, profits? What values do the owners hold toward employees?

What lines, products, services should the company handle? What customers, markets, or areas should it seek to serve? What organizational structure follows? What pricing or credit terms should be available to customers and to vendors? What sources of money will the company seek? What overall personnel policies will fit in with the market needs of the organization? For example, is customer retention based on presumed loyalty or on technical knowledge? How this last question is answered will affect *both* the selection of personnel and the compensation system.

Question 3

What information does the company need in order to make its key decisions? What is the quality of the information it depends upon and has to know in order to excel?

Information can be divided into hard and soft, external and internal. Internal information arises out of the activities of the company itself: sales, accounts receivable, costs, number of employees, and so forth. It is generally hard, that is, auditable. External information is generally soft and more difficult to obtain. But it also is more useful in directing the employment of the firm's resources. What are the attitudes of our customers? What are the strengths and weaknesses of competitors? Why don't people buy from us? What is happening in the various environments in which we operate?

Question 4

What jobs naturally develop around the need to make key decisions? Who should make the key decisions? What discretion can a salesman, an office manager, a factory manager, a warehouse manager use?

The reason for asking these kinds of questions is that in most smaller companies good jobs—jobs that offer power, flexibility, the opportunity to use one's skills to the fullest advantage—are few and we should make sure they are staffed with first-rate people. The obverse is also true: Smaller companies cannot tolerate an excessive number of good people because, if there is not enough for them to do, they will become destructive to the company.

In order to attract and retain good people, it may be necessary to fit many hats on a single individual, to assign several functions to one competent manager in order to make his job satisfying.

Question 5

What control does management need at different levels so that people are led to make the right decisions to maintain the competitive advantage, but are not inhibited by so many controls that their initiative is destroyed?

There is no one right way of setting up controls. We have to be sensitive to the manager's right *not* to know, not to be swamped with irrelevant information. We have to be careful to maintain a balance between efficiency and the ability to adapt.

Question 6

What reward system, of which money is the clearest and sharpest signal, will direct people to the results, the performances that the company wants, to maintain the competitive advantage?

We think it is crucial to underline this point, and therefore we repeat it. If a company knows why customers buy and what its competitive advantages are, and if management wants to keep and perhaps expand on the uses of those advantages, the sharpest, clearest signals it can give about what it wants are the rewards people see resulting from performance supporting the objective.

In our model the more management wants above the "normal" behavior of its people the more differently it must pay to get that performance. There is a direct relationship between differentials in attainment and compensation; the higher you set your target the more power you will have to use to get it. To achieve high aims be prepared to pay high.

Questions on Pay and Performance

In the course of administering Management Physicals® we have evolved a series of questions that touch on performance and pay. To help you use the questions in developing greater clarity in your own compensation systems, we list and discuss these questions below. The questions can be used in interviews between top management and its employees, or they can be incorporated into an employee opinion or attitude survey questionnaire to be completed anonymously by all employees, the results of which are summarized and fed back to employees. The purpose of the questions is to elicit some of the feelings that people have about their jobs and the relationship of their pay to their performance.

Why did you get your last raise? What do you have to do to earn more? What does doing a good job mean?

These questions are related. If a person does not know why he received one amount rather than another on his last raise, it is obvious that he either did not know what he had to do in order to earn more money or that the compensation program was misrepresented. Either way the company stands to lose. If a person does not know what doing a good job means, he is unable to satisfy the universal desire of most people to feel self-respect in their work; if he does not believe that he will receive the rewards held out to him for superior performance, he is not likely to try.

The questions are also designed to find out how well you are meeting people's hunger for knowing how they are doing. In our experience, the common answers to the third question indicate negative measures of performance and include such comments as:

> "No one yelled at me last week."

> "I'm still here, aren't I?"

> "If you don't do a good job around here, somebody lets you know. If you do a good job, you have to tell yourself."

No matter how well people are paid in money, they also want to be told when they have done or are doing well. While thanks cannot make up for the lack of financial reward (when it can be afforded), money cannot make up for silence following outstanding performance. Thanks cost nothing; silence devalues the rewards given. Being ignored is worse than being criticized.

Who knows how you feel about your pay and your performance?

This question seeks out the feelings of key people about their work and their pay; it probes the degree to which a company has succeeded in getting employees to identify themselves with it. How they relate their perceptions to the perceptions of the company about their pay and performance is a direct measure of the adequacy of the compensation program.

We know from hundreds of experiences that people's perceptions about why they earned what they did and why they are not earning what they think they should can be significantly different from the real reasons, and their work, consequently, can be seriously affected.

Employees should not be allowed to drift between review sessions and salary changes, unhappy over pay issues which can be discovered and explained. The approach that we suggest, therefore, is that a formal process be instituted as part of the compensation program of each smaller company to find out how people generally—and key people particularly—feel about their pay levels and raises.

The question is also used to identify the occasional person who feels he is not adequately paid. In our experience, about 85 percent of the people will feel that their raise and pay level are within a reasonable range; about 10 percent will admit, once trust has been established, that their raise was more than they expected; and about 5 percent will feel that they have been poorly handled. It is the 5 percent that we want to discover and investigate.

Following is a technique that has worked successfully: After finding out what the unhappy employee feels he should be earning, and especially why he feels he should be earning more than the amount he received, the superior promises that he will be back to the subordinate in a few days with an answer. He promises nothing in terms of amounts of money but he does promise to look into the situation.

One of the authors used this procedure as a manager for many years, and in about half the cases he adjusted the salary, occasionally for the amount requested but usually more than had been originally decided.

The background implied by this small-company compensation adjustment policy is one of openness and humility: openness, in the sense that management directly and explicitly shows that it understands how important pay is to people and that it wants to know how they feel about it; humility, in the sense that it is almost impossible to devise a compensation system which works with accuracy and justice all the time. Unfortunately, many compensation administrators feel that once a program has been set and the methods of performance measurements established, it is a sign of weakness to change a raise or reward.

Being flexible does not jeopardize the financial health of the company. Since all salary decisions fall within a range of reasonableness, if they are arrived at objectively and with an honest attempt to relate the various factors discussed in this book, it is clear that when the final figure has been arrived at and is disputed, the necessity to change the award is not likely to result in a large increment of pay or open the company to charges of lacking confidence in its pay program.

The analogy is that experienced accountants would like to issue financial statements with a range of reasonableness rather than a fixed figure because they know that, although a balance sheet balances and an income statement concludes with a single number, the "truth" lies within a range of 10 to 20 percent of the stated figures. Thus, it is possible in determining how much of a raise or reward to give that opinions will vary between an employee's and a company's perceptions of how much should be given.

If raises, bonuses, and job relationships are devised and explained from early employment as extensions of an attempt to be fair, and if the employee accepts management's decency and good intentions, it then becomes possible for both parties openly to discuss pay levels. Management can then make adjustments when information on which pay changes have been based is incorrect or evaluators have submitted inaccurate information. On the other hand, when the information is accurate, such discussion brings disappointment and, possibly, disaffection into the open.

Who gets the raises, who gets the promotions, and for what?

Pay raises may be a secret; promotions never are. If you want to know what your managers think they have to do to move ahead, this question will elicit their views of what has to be done to get ahead in your company.

In one case, five nonfamily managers in a retail chain answered this question about who received promotions by stating that only family members and those who did not argue with the president of the company moved ahead. Anyone who was not related to him or who openly disagreed with him either was fired or had quickly learned to keep quiet. This credo was not part of the personnel manual, but the promotion system had made it clear to employees what was required to rise in the organization. The reality of the situation was expressed by the comment of one manager, who said, "I'm looking for another job since the president's only remaining relative not in the company is his twelve-year-old daughter, and I can't wait for her to grow up so that I might marry her."

Which three people contribute most to the company's success? Why do you list them? Are they properly rewarded and recognized?

It is very possible for a company to improperly identify the principal contributors to the company's profits or even its survival. An open-end question such as this will reveal the quiet, steady managers upon whom the company depends who often are not valued as much as some more colorful and conspicuous ones. The answers can make sure that people are properly recognized for genuine contribution in terms of their status and pay.

Which one person would the company miss the most?

This question deals with the key producer of profits or the person who provides the lubricant which permits the organization to function effectively. It is based on the fact that employees of a company always know who the real contributors are and which among them contributes the most, independent of titles, position, or pay.

In one company which manufactures an item used in the processing and plumbing industries, the key to its success was a sixty-five-year-old engineer whose competence was such that the tasks of dealing with customers, solving technical problems, designing the special equipment required, setting prices, and scheduling deliveries fell naturally upon his shoulders. Although he had only a minor place in the organizational chart, he solved the technical problems and saw to it that the product got out on time with such speed and integrity that key customers preferred to deal with him. He was neither an officer of the company nor a stockholder; however, he was the person the company would miss the most.

After a new owner acquired the company, he acted to reduce the vulnerability of the firm's uniqueness by making the pay, retirement, and recognition systems zero in on retaining the engineer. To ensure the passing on of his special role, several younger people were assigned to back him on each key customer contact.

REVIEWING THE PRESENT PLAN AND THE ORGANIZATION

Should this be the first time you have formally designed a compensation plan, keep in mind one of the themes in this book; namely, compensation plans *always* exist. Each planning session, therefore, should begin with a search for and review of *all* the elements that influence compensation, some of which are always hidden from the casual view.

The word "plan" derives from the latin *planus,* meaning "level ground." In effect, planning starts with leveling (that is, clearing) the ground. Compensation planning clears the ground for its plans by first identifying the factors which have current influence on pay. The range and diversity of what is found are always astonishing. The items range from the warm qualities of decency, kindness, and sentimentality to the cold ones of prejudice, selfishness, and greed. Sometimes, in between, are found a few factually based influences.

In any company that wants to achieve excellence, planning is always conducted on an integrated basis. To plan compensation without tying it in with other planning efforts is wasteful. Therefore, preparation for redesigning the compensation program should always include an examination of the organization and possibly the number of changes shown by the examination to be needed. Sound management ties organization development and compensation planning together.

Smaller firms tend to have enduring organizational structures despite the fact that their key executives play more roles and operate more flexibly than those in larger firms. But the environment, which is constantly changing, requires organization to be responsive even though structural changes come more slowly than the forces that make them necessary.

Successful companies recognize the need to change their deployment of responsibilities, authority, and work assignments in the changing factors of competition, customer needs, supplies, economic conditions, the ways in which work is viewed, levels of pay, and techniques in motivating and satisfying people. *"The ideal organization is a tent, not a temple."*

One of the purposes of compensation planning is to make the environment of the key manager more realistic, to engender clear understanding of what is expected, and by setting priorities, to offset the fracturing effects of time pressures. Also, certain kinds of results take longer to bring to fruition than conventional bookkeeping accounts for. Research and development projects, major capital expenditures, management development, and strengthened market share are managerial tasks for which the normal annual income statement is inadequate.

USING JOB EVALUATION SYSTEMS AND SALARY SURVEYS

Companies often use job evaluation methods in forming (and maintaining) compensation systems. Such systems are primarily

*From Bo L. T. Hedberg, Paul C. Nystrom, and William H. Starbuck, "Camping on Seesaws: Prescriptions for a Self-Designing Organization,"*Administrative Science Quarterly,* March 1976.

useful in fixing base pay, although they also serve usefully to clarify job and organizational structure. We find the methods to be helpful in small business. An example of a job evaluation program devised for a $4-million company by one of the authors is in Appendix I.

Conducting Your Own Compensation Survey

Where communication is open and managers feel comfortable expressing their feelings about pay, fringe benefits, and working conditions, the feedback needed for top managers to update and fine-tune their compensation programs is not much of a problem. In such companies, regular annual dialogues (salary review, performance review, or combination of the two) usually take place anyway.

When the atmosphere is closed and feelings are repressed and you want to know quickly what attitudes managers hold, consider conducting a survey designed for the purpose. We have used the sample in Appendix II frequently. Adapt it to your company's needs and use it with the assurance it will be helpful.

Be sure the survey provides anonymity, and feed back the results in at least summary form to the particpants. Where substantial deficiencies are revealed, be open and report the action you plan to take. Even better results may come from an employee task force.

If the fringe benefit program or information system is criticized, useful improvements may be suggested by a group of concerned managers who are assigned the job of coming up with specific suggestions. If total cost limits are set, the group can adjust the benefits to their taste and need.

Using Prepared Salary Surveys

Salary surveys are produced in this country by the thousands: by associations, consultants, government agencies, and quasi-public institutions such as chambers of commerce. Most of them are of little help to smaller firms because the surveys do little more than relate compensation to sales volume and specific titles in an organization. Since executives are more often paid for handling sales volume than for managing assets and producing profits, the data tend to follow and also reinforce that practice. More meaningful data would relate salaries also to contribution to profits.

If the salary of a valued executive does not fall, as it seems it should, within a given survey salary range, there is little choice but to consider his compensation from the viewpoint of profit contribution. For example, if three executives running $7-million-a-year equipment dealerships earn $60,000, $100,000, and $125,000, respectively, we have to look beyond the sales figures to the profit earned to account for the disparity. The higher the company's profits and the greater your responsibility for these profits, the more you are entitled to earn.

As to job titles, they do not describe the inputs or outputs of jobs. Presidents, sales managers, or controllers do not do the same thing in all companies, whatever their size. Only in extremely large organizations with precise job definitions (assistant controllers in a national retailer's regional offices, or branch managers for large insurance companies) are the same job results expected.

In smaller companies, a chief executive normally handles at least one major function in addition to his CEO role. To the extent that his job includes profit-making responsibility not handled by another person holding a title normal to the role, he should be compensated. Examples include the CEO who is also the major salesman, or handles all financial deals, or does the screening, training, and personnel job.

Large jumps in pay within a single year may be justified in companies which could not pay adequate or fair salaries in the past. When the company has a good year the reasonableness of the increase must be measured against inflation compounded from the date when salaries were frozen and inadequate in comparison with local or industry standards.

ASSURING ACCEPTANCE OF THE PLAN

To achieve effectiveness in compensation planning, you must assure the plan's acceptance, and that is best achieved by assuring objectivity. Here is a legitimate place for a committee. Consider a committee of three to seven people (management appointed or elected) to set salary *levels* (not individual pay) for levels below top management. A committee experience, which builds up the group, can also advise as to the *number* of salary levels and steps within each salary level.

Gaining acceptance of the plan can also be achieved by attending to the quality of documentation. Certainly, the firm that wishes to get the most mileage out of its compensation plan will see that it is packaged in an attractive, complete, clearly written, simple, flexible manual (so papers can be easily replaced).

Eschew secrecy; give the manual to every employee and explain the system used (point-factor for job evaluation or other kind) to determine relativity between salary levels. Since some of the most vexing compensation problems originate in the comparisons employees make between what pay they and others receive and what they believe they and others should receive, it is worth considering making the basic compensation plan available to everyone in the firm. Specifically, consider disclosure of salary levels but not individual pay. The small problems that will arise will probably be less than those you'll have if you keep salary levels secret.

If a pay plan is offered humbly as not being the last word and is maintained with a sensitivity for change as circumstances warrant, you can handle the nit-picking that is likely to follow.

APPRAISING PERFORMANCE

A strong, objective performance evaluation system cannot be installed by degrees. It is like the planning process; if an organization decides to run its operations on the basis of planning rather than reaction, it cannot install planning in small doses. If a doctor tells you to exercise every day but you exercise only three times a week, you are probably improving your health more than if you exercised not at all. But planning for an overall organization and a performance evaluation system cannot be done in partial doses. Either you plan or you do not plan; otherwise, you create chaos. Either have a performance evaluation system under which you hand out raises, bonuses, and promotions, or have none.

Salary changes should be made only for reasons that are honestly and candidly given. That accords with our view that people should always know what they must do to earn more. To give increases or withhold them *without* justification negates the principle of more pay for more results. Performance appraisal and compensation adjustments are therefore, in our view, inseparable. Even when giving a raise is not justified by performance, appraisal is useful.

Evaluation of performance should precede salary review by a

fair amount of time. A benefit is that a supervisor who knows that the work of a subordinate is below standard can so notify the subordinate before salary change time. If the subordinate's salary is not changed, the withholding comes as less of a shock.

Evaluation includes both pay and the opportunity of promotion which brings higher pay. It is usually easier to determine that an employee is ready for a promotion than it is to justify a merit increase within a job. The reason is that merit rate changes often have gray area differences, whereas job responsibility differences (with different pay) are clearer and easier to determine.

One of the most difficult problems in performance appraisal is dealing with the differences between how people think they are doing and how they are actually doing. In several studies of the subject no one rated himself below the fiftieth percentile; in other studies only a small percentage of employees rated themselves below the seventy-fifth percentile.

Since we know that both talent and performance are normally distributed in most organizations, the differences between how people perceive they are doing and how they are actually doing will cause problems. If they are not paid in accordance with their perceptions (even granting that the perceptions are put forth for reasons aside from honest self-appraisal), problems will arise; if they are paid in accordance with their perceptions, the company more often than not is reinforcing unproductive behavior.

Merit Raises

Although many organizations have an announced policy that pay increases are distributed on merit, employees often see the increases as based on seniority rather than ability, on the cost of living, or some narrow formula which disregards individual differences in contribution. If everyone receives a 5 percent raise, or even if three levels of increases are used, say 10 percent for good performance, 6 percent for average, and 3 percent for something better than merely adequate, you hurt most the individual whose performance does not fit neatly into any category—the outstanding performer, the one you most want or need to retain.

A better idea, if the organization is small enough, is to fashion individual pay programs for your key management people. That is practical for groups up to 20 in number. Individualized programs become an increasing burden above that size.

Many people assume that a merit increase is based on the following steps: (1) The manager appraises the performance of his subordinate and gives a raise (or not) within financial or personnel manual guidelines; (2) the manager informs the employee of the performance appraisal and the amount of his increase, if any; (3) the employee substantially agrees with the basis of the performance evaluation; and (4) in order to perform better and earn more money, the employee changes his performance.

The facts, which also cause the problems in merit appraisal, are probably more along the following lines:

1. The manager decides on the amount of the raise he wants to give and then justifies or creates the appraisal to fit his financial decision. He uses the typical sandwich approach in his appraisal: first a compliment, then a criticism, then a slap-on-the-back compliment to send the employee off. The performance appraisal has been made to fit the financial (the pay) decision.

2. Factors other than performance or merit determine the political decision to give a raise:

Seniority.
Peer relationships.
Inflation.
The place of the employee within a predetermined range.

Employees are not deceived by the foregoing stratagems; they are very practical in their understanding of the influences that shape their pay. Many of them are aware when an evalution system is superficial or a management trapping without substance, especially when it does not separate performance levels. And when the system is superficial, they accept seniority, inflation, and similar reasons as reasonable bases for setting their pay. But the inevitable result is that the compensation system of the smaller company loses all its power to direct and motivate behavior.

3. Employees properly question the validity of the rating: How fairly do the evaluators appraise the performance? Most companies not only have inadequate appraisal systems, but they do not try to find out how those appraised feel about the appraisals and, therefore, how, or whether, they will change their behavior.

In the experience of the authors, if the results of an appraisal system are to be useful they must not only be challengeable but must also be filtered and edited by top management's knowledge of the objectivity of the evaluators. A merit system is not a mechanical affair. It relies almost totally upon the competence of the evaluators; it can be no better than their qualifications. In one company several evaluators felt that all those beneath them should be fired, whereas other evaluators felt that all those beneath *them* were extraordinary and deserved large promotions and raises. Both groups were wrong.

4. Few appraisals are oriented toward job results. More often the ratings are based on such traits as friendliness, helpfulness, loyalty, and intelligence, which not only are hard to define but are often totally irrelevant to the performance.

5. Merit raises usually fall within a narrow range, sometimes as small as 5 to 8 percent of the previous salary. But performance results spread over a much wider range. When employees see the difference between the two ranges, those who might possibly be motivated to change their performance by rewards in proportion to results are quickly turned off.

6. It is hard to set job performance standards of equal quality for different jobs and sample salary levels. Therefore, the quality of appraisals (between jobs) is not consistent. Jobs which have a strong element of qualitative results—training, cleanliness, relationship with customers and vendors—are especially difficult. In such jobs we tend to measure those things which we find more on the surface, such as hard work, loyalty, intelligence, long hours, rather than specific results.

As a final distortion of the merit system, if you react to the outside world in terms of competitive salaries to key people, if you are somewhat sensitive to inflation, and if you pay according to education, experience, scarcity of job, danger, pressure, longevity, or some obvious standard, you will probably keep most people happy. However, you will not retain the outstanding performers, and your pay system will not motivate (again, change the behavior of) people by relating rewards and performance.

At least this system will be peace-keeping, and you will not be discouraging the many employees who find that pay is a maintenance as opposed to a motivating aspect of their work. You might, under this peace-keeping mode, set aside 5 to 10 percent of your total pay increases for the extraordinary performers and give them amounts related in some way to their superior performance. You may keep the good ones and you will not alienate the 90 percent of the ordinary, adequate performers.

Another technique might be to divide your people into marginal, competent, and exceptional groups and give different amounts of raises to each group on some predetermined basis. Once again, this will be a peace-keeping, not an individualized, motivating pay program.

When it is done without a clear understanding of performance standards and pay, salary administration cannot be more than an extension of financial control. It becomes an area of conflict between management's desires to achieve results and its concern for salary dollars on the one hand, and the needs of good people to know where they stand and be rewarded for specific performance on the other.

Emphasis on Results, Not Traits

We have referred to the problems stemming from evaluating traits and have emphasized that it is results or output that a small-company compensation system should be concerned with. We are seduced by our normal interest in other human beings and in talking or gossiping about their obvious traits.

How does one define an aggressive salesman, a loyal clerk, an intelligent controller? The word "aggressive" means different things to different people. For an unsure buyer an aggressive salesman would be convincing; to a person who really knows what he wants an aggressive salesman would be annoying; to someone not quite sure an astute salesman can be supportive and convincing.

What does "loyal" mean? In one company in which internal thievery was a major problem, the president defined a loyal employee as one who did not steal *much*. In another company employees were considered loyal if they did not complain about their pay and did what they were asked to do. Rarely was it a person who worked for the company's interest as opposed to his own personal interest.

A second issue revolves around the ability and propriety of management to try to change the traits of those working under them. Does the smaller-company manager who has the ability *and* the obligation to create a consistent and motivating working atmosphere have the right to tamper with the personality of a subordinate through a performance evaluation reward system, even if his intent is not to be manipulative but to improve satisfaction on the job and the earnings of the subordinate? We feel it is neither right nor practical.

There are only a few ways personality can change: religious conversion, psychiatry, neurosurgery, drugs, or massive psychological trauma. None of these is appropriate to the small-business atmosphere.

We sympathize with the frustration of the manager who knows that an employee is capable of performing differently but doesn't. The manager's job is rather to help his subordinates develop and do what they are best at and to ease out those whose interests and capabilities do not fit corporate needs.

Performance evaluation should not be conducted as a psychological investigation. It has only two objectives: (1) to determine how well responsibilities have been fulfilled and should be rewarded (if at all), and (2) over time, to determine whether or not the person is in the right job or line of work.*

Performance starts with selection. There is no reward system that will make a person do certain things if the individual is intellectually or psychologically incapable of satisfying the needs of the job. You cannot and should not try to create rewards which will make him change his personality.

A simple example from the experience of one of the authors: During his army career, he was a battalion sergeant major when an opening occurred among the officers for a warrant officership for which he was an obvious and probably the sole qualified candidate. Because the sergeant did not like the lieutenant colonel in charge of the battalion, he had to make the decision as to whether his wish to be a warrant officer would be more than offset by his distaste for having to socialize as an officer with the colonel. He decided to reject the warrant officership.

Think of a position or profession in which you are *not* interested. Is there any reward which will induce you to perform at a high level in that profession?

One of the authors was once asked whether he would like to be a dentist. He said that he was grateful there were people who enjoyed dentistry because when he had a toothache he would rather have an

*See Robert Mager and Peter Pipe, *Analyzing Performance Problems* (Belmont, Calif: Fearon, 1970).

interested dentist than a tennis player take care of him. On the other hand, there was absolutely nothing that could get *him* to be a dentist.

To summarize, if you want high performance, make sure that the person you have engaged for the job is capable of it, that he has the right intellectual skills, emotional maturity, interests, and that the results you want will be considered worthy of his efforts. Without the right aptitude, there is no training or organizational environment that will effectively change behavior.

We suggest the use of a local professional industrial psychologist and the use of tests where they are relevant (usually where there is an obvious connection between job demands and particular competences, such as mathematical ability in actuaries, language ability in copyeditors).

Group interviews can improve the productivity of the selection process. In this procedure, all the managers who will have contact with the applicant meet with him at the same time. To avoid chaos, one person is designated to carry the bulk of the interview and asks prearranged questions. The last half of the interview is an open session where anyone present can ask questions.

After each applicant has been interviewed, the group lists his strong and weak points. These are then communicated to the several applicants, who are asked to prepare answers for a second group interview. At the end of the second interview, it is usually fairly easy to determine who is the best applicant.

We recommend that you spend a disproportionate amount of your time in checking references. If we assume that most human behavior is consistent, the best projection of what an applicant will do is what he has done. We have found that successful reference checking requires persistence and imagination, as well as a good deal of effort.

One of the most thorough reference-checking procedures we have ever seen was done by a personnel agency that was searching for a personnel manager for a medium-size company. The agency checked not only the applicant's superiors for the last fifteen years, but customers for whom he had worked, his peers, and at least a half dozen of his subordinates. Twelve references were obtained which, when analyzed, yielded the client company a full picture of the applicant's performance.

5

Designing
the Plan

HAVING cleared the ground and built the foundation for planning, you are now ready to create the plan itself. This chapter lays down and discusses the basic steps in that process.

TYPES OF PAY

We have dealt so far in this book with many of the variables which affect what people are paid and what they want from pay. Now it is time to consider pay itself, to describe its different forms and how each can be used to serve a company's interests.

There are five basic ways in which compensation can be paid to managers. It is important to see them for their different purposes since they serve different needs and are viewed by managers in different ways. We will summarize them and then investigate each in more detail.

Salary, or base pay. Salary is the amount regularly paid for doing a good (or at least "standard") job daily. It is usually related to competitive factors in the outside world, and for most managers (about 75 per cent, according to one study) is the single most important part of their pay.

A variable incentive bonus. Part of a compensation package paid to a small group of executives with key positions, this bonus is for achieving specific objectives. It is usually short-term, measurable to at least a fair degree, and probably the single most important motivator of the total compensation package.

Long-term or capital accumulation. Because most managers have not accepted Social Security as an adequate means of paying employees who have spent the bulk of their working lives with a company, pension plans, profit-sharing plans, and other means of capital accumulation are used to reward the long-term employee and to permit the building of an estate through the tax-saving devices that the IRS has encouraged. Because the number of key executives in smaller companies is few, it is possible to negotiate individual plans to satisfy individual needs. Deferred compensation contracts, shadow stock or stock appreciation rights, and capital stock distribution through sale, gift, or bonus are some of the techniques available.

Benefits. These are the fixed costs portion of pay and are primarily aimed at protecting employees from catastrophe. Benefits are seldom directly related to performance, although some of them increase with salary and organizational levels. Today they are so common they are regarded as necessities and due, and are therefore largely nonmotivating. Differences in benefits hardly ever cause movement from one company to another.

Perquisites. These are the individualized cash and noncash benefits that set executives as a group and as individuals apart. "Perks" are usually modest in cost but high in motivational value. The costs are kept in check by IRS rules of reasonableness, but the range and quality of perquisities are sufficient to be prized and sought by most executives.

BASE PAY

Designing a compensation plan starts with a review of the existing salary structure from the viewpoint of adequacy (externally) and equity (internally).

Base pay is what employees can be sure of receiving, and usually falls between 50 percent and 80 percent of the total compensation package. Therefore, it also is the benchmark by which they measure how they are perceived in the outside world and by their companies and other employees, how they judge the suitability of an outside job offer, and so forth. When an individual is considering taking a job with you, base pay is the main yardstick he uses to compare with the job he is leaving or has left. It strongly flavors the quality of company life and sets the standard and style of family living.

Setting the right base pay starts with an examination of organizational needs—how many specialties you need, how many levels are needed to control decision making, what you must do especially well in your business to succeed. Few industries change overnight; therefore, changing demands for skills can be identified in a systematic, timely manner only through a thorough and objective review of what the company must do well and the skills entailed to do so. Since the needs of firms usually change long before their organizational structures, and since smaller companies are particularly lax in anticipating their future job needs, the review of base pay offers a unique opportunity to deal with the vagueness of the future. (See "Analyzing the Business" in Chapter 4.)

After you have identified the needs, the next step is to see what others are paying for the skills to meet those needs. Sources of information on the competitive adequacy of pay are compensation surveys, classified advertisements in the leading business and local papers, professional personnel-finding agencies, your accounting firm (if it does recruiting), and your trade or professional associations, which usually keep tabs on going salary rates. A tough-minded review of the reasons you have lost good people (have they left for significant differences in base pay?) will also be informative.

In focusing on other forms of compensation don't make the mistake of underestimating the importance of base pay to even the most gifted employees. Of course, the significance of base pay in the compensation package relates to the maturity of most managers in dealing with their own finances. But for most, fixed base pay sets the living standard; only irresponsible executives depend upon and live up to their bonus level. Mature executives usually see themselves as $20,000-, $50,000-, or $100,000-a-year people. They expect to continue earning at least the equivalent of their base pay, and they therefore plan where they will live, the size house they occupy, the vacations and schooling they can handle, and other elements of their basic lifestyle in terms of that expectation. Furthermore, they also know that base pay affects other forms of compensation such as pension, insurance, and some bonus plans.

The local market is the usual range setter for base pay. These levels work in two ways: Managers know they are entitled to but cannot expect more than the reasonable ranges for the size of company and type of job they have. By the same token, the company management knows it cannot attract or retain people if it goes below the floor, nor does it need to pay base wages higher than the local ceilings.

Base pay is not merely a reward for doing work at a given level well; it can also be used to stimulate rises in performance levels and self-development. If people know what they can earn if they are promoted, and that the earnings differences are major, base pay can act as a strong motivator. Therefore, don't have too many pay levels in the salary structure. If levels are compressed, as they often are in small companies where differences between jobs are often slight, then salary levels will be a demotivator.

Most people underestimate the pay of those above them and overestimate the pay of those below them when, in both cases, they do not know the facts. These inaccurate perceptions of the difference in salary levels speak strongly for open disclosure of salary levels.

Although a well-grounded review of base pay is almost certain to yield benefits, don't be swept away by the results; be conservative in changing present pay scales. People are jealous of their place in the pay heirarchy, and the more the relationships are changed the greater is the likelihood of major disturbances. Limit yourself to making fine adjustments in the existing scale unless the company undergoes major reorganization or has suffered such serious problems that any moves for survival are acceptable.

Setting Salary Levels and Differentials

Salaries should be set at levels which are adequate for the basic living needs of key people to free them from most financial concerns. Admittedly, that is not easy to do because subjective views of what is adequate and what basic needs are get in the way. Therefore, salaries should err on the high side of what it takes to live comfortably. If that can be accomplished only by keeping a lid on staffing that is not necessarily damaging. It is better to have one less employee on the payroll than to pay key people on the low side.

Our experience suggests the wisdom of being generous in setting base salaries. A quotation from our earlier book, *Survival & Growth,* may be appropriate in setting the place of people costs:

> Few small company managers see the possession of competitively compensated technical and management skills as a business advantage. The others have held to the view, arising out of the first struggles of a newly formed and thinly financed company, that all things—including personnel—should be bought as cheaply as possible.
>
> Such a view is neither necessary nor economically justified. In the long run it forces the firm to rely on second-rate employees and overlook problems such as low productivity, employee indifference, and inability to grow, which are symptoms of an inadequate organization. The evidence bearing on manpower strongly supports the view that small firms will profit from spending money for good people at every level and treating people as an inherently rich resource.*

Comments on this point of view, extended to the setting of salaries for new positions or for recruitment purposes, are contained in Appendix I.

The first step in establishing a salary matrix is to find out the market value of various skills. Those can be obtained from trade associations that perform salary surveys, the Financial Executive Institute, the Research Insitute of America, the American Management Associations Compensation Service, and occasionally, by reference to the giant corporations in the same industry. Executive search and personnel agencies and newspaper advertisements are other sources. The salary ranges of publicly held companies may often be so much greater than that affordable by or relevant to the smaller company that they may not seem to have any value. But published statistics can help determine compensation relationships between jobs, as well as actual salary ranges for jobs.

Be careful in using survey data. In many cases the number of

---

*Theodore Cohn and Roy A. Lindberg, *Survival & Growth: Management Strategies for the Small Firm* (New York: AMACOM, 1974).

respondents for a sales volume range is so small that distortions occur. Moreover, the surveys are rarely based on valid statistical sampling principles. Companies volunteer to participate; thus, a particular survey may be slanted in favor of high- or low-salaried executives or in favor of high- or low-profit companies. In addition, although executive titles may be the same from company to company, what the executives actually do may differ widely.

The problem of what is a CEO, a vice-president of sales or manufacturing, and so on, is especially difficult in smaller companies where it is common for an executive to wear many hats. As an example, take the functions of the CEO in a group of supermarkets or equipment distributorships, two industries with which the authors have had particular experience. The CEO in both performs a wide range of functions in addition to those traditionally assigned to him. In a distributorship the CEO may be not only the chief administrative or operating officer but also the chief salesman, the major contact with factories, and the chief personnel officer. In another distributorship the CEO may serve only in an executive function, and may not handle sales directly or have any direct contact with factories. His major concern may be financial.

The range of the jobs assumed by supermarket CEO's is probably as great. Some we have known are immediately concerned with marketing strategies and with merchandising; others have little to do with it. Some are deeply involved in finance; others have first-rate financial officers and have nothing to do with that function but concentrate on personnel.

Finally, almost all surveys limit their data to breakdowns of industries and sales volume. We feel strongly that executives should not be paid for handling or creating sales or any other operating function but for producing overall results or profits. Since few surveys connect the profitability of the reporting companies with salary levels by industry and volume, the executive whose performance has resulted in extraordinary profits has no way of measuring his proper salary against those who have also performed extraordinarily. He can relate his salary only to volume levels.

In several consulting experiences, we have gone beyond surveys to the information available in proxy statements. By adding data on profitability to data on volume and industry we have been able to develop a sounder range of reasonableness for the extraordinary performer. However, even this technique has substantial limits since it is onerous to pick out the proxy statements for small, comparable publicly held companies whose results are above average.

How can closely held company executives reach agreement on how much each is worth in relation to the others? The first step is to set the salary of the chief executive or the most important person in the company (as described below). We then can move from that benchmark to the relationship of the other executives. We have found the following technique practical:

A group of executives who are to be evaluated are asked to submit a list to an outsider (CPA, attorney, consultant) in which they rank each member of the group, including themselves, in terms of value to the company, ability to contribute to profits, how much will be missed if gone. The rankings are then reconciled by the outsider. (The reason for using an outsider is that the group has to continue to work and live with each other; it serves no useful purpose for one executive to learn how others rated him.)

In almost all cases, we have found that there is extraordinary agreement on where each member of the group should stand. In one case where nine executives were asked to perform the ranking, everyone was ranked within one place of his mode (the most commonly agreed upon number).

After the ranking is done, the individuals are asked to place each member of the group is some percentage relationship to the Number 1 person, who is set at 100 percent. The ranking does not separate levels since each person is separated by a single digit of equal value. In the ranking we assume that the difference in value or contribution is the same between the persons ranked 1 and 2 and the persons ranked 2 and 3. If this were true, it would be coincidental and rare. We ask the proportion question to get some idea of the true relationships.

With the percentage evaluations in hand, the outsider can then take the comparative salary ratings obtained from outside sources and draft a first salary proportion plan, or an executive can use the summary findings without knowing who rated whom.

Example. Assume a top executive group of seven people are asked to rank themselves in order of profit contribution. The results are shown in Figures 1 and 2.

Figure 1. Number of times ranked (mode is circled).

	1	2	3	4	5	6	7
Brown	(5)	2					
Jones	2	(4)	1				
Smith		1	(5)	1			
Dobson				(5)	1	1	
Harkin			1	1	(4)		1
Gale					1	(5)	1
Palen					1	1	(5)

Figure 2. Results of proportion question.

Ranked by

	Brown	Jones	Smith	Dobson	Harkin	Gale	Palen	Total	Average
Brown	100	95	100	100	100	95	100	690	99
Jones	80	100	75	75	80	100	70	580	83
Smith	60	65	70	80	75	60	60	470	67
Dobson	50	55	65	70	75	60	55	430	61
Harkin	45	45	60	70	60	65	60	405	58
Gale	45	50	55	50	45	50	55	350	50
Palen	40	50	45	50	40	50	45	320	46

Salary surveys show a range of $70,000 to $120,000 for the base pay of top executives of companies in the same industry and of approximately comparable size. Because the company's ROI is on the low side of the average, a target figure of $85,000 is set. As a first test of reasonableness, the other executives' salaries are then slotted into a relationship with $85,000 using the average proportion percentage (Table 1).

Table 1. Actual and ideal executive salary scale.

	Percentage	Ideal Amount	Present Salary
Brown	99	$85,000	$90,000
Jones	83	70,500	80,000
Smith	67	57,000	60,000
Dobson	61	52,000	55,000
Harkin	58	49,300	50,000
Gale	50	42,500	45,000
Palen	46	39,000	35,000

A heavy dose of sensitivity and taste is now prescribed to bring present salaries in line with the ideal relationships. Normally, the adjustments are handled by giving raises only where applicable but not reducing salaries.

When several manager-stockholders have equal stock interest in the company and are paid equal salaries, varying perceptions of who contributes how much to profit causes problems, especially for the most effective manager-stockholder, who most feels the inequity. A first step in solving the problem can be to set fair basic salaries tied to competitive local standards for each stockholder's job. An outsider's recommendations for separating responsibility and contribution (based on the ranking procedure), when acceptable, lend objectivity to the procedure. Without acceptance of the propriety of different pay for different work, an equal stockholder relationship may never move off dead center and the problems arising from equality of pay and inequality of contribution may never cease. And the problems are not to be treated lightly; they often become the principal drag on a smaller company's ability to progress to better results.

Beware of the compensation consultant who does not talk with those affected by a compensation plan. It is almost impossible to set up a compensation program that will satisfy the standards listed at the beginning of this book if it does not include the input of the people who know the company best and will have to live with the program. Not only are managers sources of information to the consultant, but if he has the time, he will wisely ask subordinates for their rankings of people who contribute to profit. Many lower-level employees have deep insight as to who really produces the results of the company. In our view, it is essential to have this information when designing a compensation program.

The Limitations of Merit Pay

Merit pay is often used to reward key people. Its limitations are its tendency toward bias, inadequate information on the part of the supervisor who disburses it, and evaluations which tend to substantiate rather than determine salary changes.

Merit raises are not for key people. When the raises are less than expected they have a negative effect. Merit pay is often confused with length of time on the job. Don't pay people for staying with the firm: They do that for themselves, not for you. When pay is tied to nonperformance items, such as longevity or education, it tends to result in buying contentment and security rather than in building the business.

Many employees relate salary increases to seniority, the profitability of the company, the economics of the outside world, their place on the company's salary scale, and the pay of others. Pay programs that are based on these factors alone, that do not in any way relate pay and performance, will serve some of the needs of some employees but not the needs of a company that wishes to excel.

When merit increases are within a narrow range and do not separate differences in performance, consider setting aside an amount from your budgeted salary increases (5 to 10 percent) for the exceptional performers. The routine performers will not miss the 5 or 10 percent, but the star performers will appreciate the extra bonus.

One of the more subtle problems of merit pay is its built-in demotivating factor. The great majority of technical and managerial employees rate their own performance in the top 10 or 20 percent. What do these unrealistic self-evaluations mean in firms with merit pay? Simply this: since payroll dollars available for merit pay or performance bonuses are limited, most employees will be consistently disappointed by their pay increases. Objective analyses of performance would in most cases show a few key people performing extremely well, most doing an adequate job, and a few performing marginally.

The most common reaction of key people to the disappointment in not receiving the pay increase they think they deserve is to downgrade the importance of their contributions and to be turned off rather than work harder to disprove the evaluation.

VARIABLE INCENTIVE BONUSES

The quality of base pay is critical to maintaining organizational stability and overall productivity. But it is the hope of incremental income that sends effort and imagination to their highest flights.

The most important considerations in creating effective bonuses is to make them variable and measurable and to see that they are paid only to those who earn them. They should not be salary substitutes. Setting up bonuses in this way is based on the assumption that the recipients are mature, do not depend on bonuses to set their lifestyle, and are willing to earn varying amounts in some proportion to varying personal achievements and corporate results.

Most incentive bonuses are selective rather than inclusive, although we will give examples of successful bonus programs that included all employees. Selective bonuses are limited because it is hard to determine the individual contribution of employees below the top level.

Bonuses Keyed to Risk

Incentive bonuses should be keyed to risk. Different industries and different jobs offer the opportunity to earn different levels of bonuses. Advertising, public relations, and women's high-style garment businesses generally face higher short-term risks than the utility, life insurance, and banking industries. The methods of paying executives in the two groups of industries also differ—executives in the higher-risk group are offered much higher incentive pay than those in the lower.

Within a company, jobs also differ in the risks that can be taken and the influence an individual's decisions have on results. Staff positions rarely have the same exposure to error as does the top executive. For example, in one company the two stockholder-principals held different positions. One was the president, whose every move was visible and whose mistakes were those of commission; the other stockholder-manager was a salesman whose successes were visible but whose failures—the inability to create a customer or make a sale—were not recorded. We had to convince the members of the small board of directors as well as the salesman-stockholder that the CEO deserved a different incentive bonus because of his job.

The reward system bears heavily on the quality of risk taking in a company. Although a business profits from taking risks, most managers try to avoid risks—to please their boss. They concentrate on what the boss wants; they try to make their boss look good because it helps them look good. Whatever the issue, they avoid conflict because it may result in a win or lose situation. The company with too many such managers is in danger of its life.

A company can use its reward system to promote and raise the quality of risk taking (that is, raise the probabilities that only good risks will be taken and the chances that the risks will be overcome). Here are some of the steps management can take:

1. State corporate and major objectives clearly, so that political or selfish behavior stands out from corporate risk-taking behavior. In smaller companies it is hard to disguise management actions. People who act for their self-interest at the expense of the company find it hard to hide.

2. Merge the goals of the company with those of individual employees to the extent possible. Getting them to jibe, even roughly, is one of the toughest management tasks and requires openness of information, participation in setting goals, and negotiations on rewards. In the rare cases when it takes place the merger has profound effects and can produce a new management style.

3. Assign responsibilities and authorities as precisely as possible so that results can be associated with individuals. Organization is important here—divide the work to be done into "wholes" so that contribution stands out as a "piece" with a beginning and an end.

4. Use an evaluation system to "trigger" the rewards the company gives for the results it wants. Give rewards proportionate to results. An example would be an incremental incentive compensation program related to return on investment. As the company's results increased over a minimum ROI, participating executives who had made identifiable contributions would be eligible for an increasing share of the profits over the base.

5. Put specifications of the performance expected of each manager in writing to minimize the chances of subjectivism, unrealistic expectations, misunderstanding, and ignorance of what is wanted.

6. Reward contributory risk taking and initiative quickly, dramatically, and significantly. The recommendation follows the Skinnerian theory that when one reinforces the desired performance, the chances of its being repeated are greatly increased. Reinforcement takes place when the rewards for acceptable behavior are considered

worthwhile and are given immediately after the desired performance has taken place.

7. Finally, start the move toward improved risk taking at the top. Defensive, political, and other forms of non-risk-taking behavior almost always spread from the top. Separate the risk takers at the top from all others and provide for significant rewards.

Bonuses Keyed to Performance

If bonuses are to have incentive value, they must be coupled with appraisals of performance against objectives set in advance. We have noted in smaller companies the rarity both of objective setting and independent appraisals. The rarities provide the opportunity to create a competitive advantage and to reach for excellence in performance.

Incentive bonuses generally range from 10 percent to 50 percent of base salary. Some are limited to a percentage of base pay, others are unlimited except as the IRS may raise a question of reasonableness. There are two basic schools of thought on setting limits for incentive bonuses:

The argument for limitation: A person will not work twice as hard for twice the money. Most executives operate normally at 70–80 percent of capacity and in many cases cannot be motivated to do better for monetary reasons only. Therefore, why offer an incentive program which permits an executive to earn 100 percent of his basic salary when for 50 percent he would put out the same effort?

The argument for no ceiling: The efforts of a manager can create profits without limit to the stockholders. Why, therefore, should the manager who creates those profits have a limit on his compensation?

In our opinion, incentive bonuses should be without limit. But they should, as in all other major business plans, be based on the realities of business life. That means they should never be paid out of the funds needed to keep the firm alive *except* when it becomes the means for keeping the company alive. And that seldom will be the case; we can think of no case where a company survived solely on the basis of paying bonuses. In the discussion later in the chapter of the formulas for incentive bonuses, we will underline this point. However, the shadow of the Internal Revenue Service stands over the compensation program of the closely held company and we will have to be sensitive to those problems. (See Chapter 6.)

Two basic decisions must be addressed when setting up bonus plans: how much is to be put into the bonus fund and how is it to be divided? The answers for the most part derive from the objectives set. Incentives cannot have meaning within themselves; they acquire it from the quality of that which they focus effort upon. Therefore, they should support company objectives. Without such objectives it is almost impossible for performance appraisals to direct managers in the right way. For example, how important is each of the following to the performance of salespersons or sales managers (we assume that salespeople cannot work on all these tasks simultaneously):

Attain a quota sales volume.
Reduce selling costs.
Obtain new accounts.
Maintain or upgrade customer goodwill.
Introduce new products.
Sell high-margin products (emphasize high-margin dollars rather than sale dollars).
Obtain a larger share of the market.
Sell more to each customer.
Perform nonselling jobs: collect and feed back information, monitor competitors, collect receivables, develop repair or service business.

Before an incentive program for salespeople or a sales manager is set up, top management should decide what its objectives are in having a salesforce. We know that sales personnel cannot operate in a vacuum, that is, without understandable guidelines to balance the tasks listed above plus tasks that their company might have in addition. It is therefore essential that a salesperson know when sales dollars are not as important as new customers, when high-margin sales are more important than sheer volume, or that he will be paid for collecting information.

Instead of dealing with the setting of objectives in any detail here, since the literature on management by objectives is so large, we list the following examples of the type of performance standards we think might be helpful in working up the bases of a performance appraisal. First of all, we will need to determine some key questions to set performance standards:

How much?
How well?
By when?
At what cost?
With what accuracy?
As compared with what?
In cooperation with whom?
What results do you want?
Can they be measured?

Next, we will have to devise some questions to ask people about their jobs to help us set performance standards. Some examples of this are: What current activities do you handle? For each activity, why do you follow a certain procedure? What results are you aiming for? How do you measure them?

Standards of performance can be positive, negative, or zero. They can also be historical, market-oriented, or engineered. (Negative standards are implicit standards, because when you know what you *don't* want you are setting as firm a standard as when you know what you *do* want. Some departments, such as service, will have more negative standards than others, like sales. Some examples of negative standards are: no customers lost, no penalties for late tax returns, or no financial statements submitted later than three working days after the end of the period.) In setting standards, be sure to avoid vague words such as "adequately," "approximate," "maximum," "minimum," "as soon as," "reasonable," "desirable," "few," or "many."

All these examples of performance standards yield reasonably to measurement. Unfortunately, many of the standards set for corporate or individual performance cannot successfully by measured. It is hard, for example, to measure management development, quality of banker relationships, acceptance by vendors and customers, or the ability to get along with people. Many services and staff functions resist having performance standards laid against them.

In a supermarket, for instance, managers do not agree on how to measure such areas of a job as store cleanliness, treatment of customers, design of merchandise display, development of people to prepare for expansion, and the causes of personnel turnover where they are attributable to a manager. These factors eventually have an impact on the income statement, but to isolate and identify them as performance standards is difficult.

We recommend that, where the results of output of an individual manager are controllable but difficult to measure, the superior use regular (daily or weekly) feedback and measure in simple three- or five-level terms such as acceptable, superior, and unacceptable. When the formal annual evaluation session takes place, the subordinate should not be surpised, if he has been receiving regular feedback.

How Individual Managers Affect ROI

In trying to relate performance to pay, keep in mind that financial statement effects may be very different from those implied by the organizational chart.

Several years ago Julius Irving, the great basketball player, moved from the New York Nets, who were playing in Long Island, to the Philadelphia 76'ers. The frankfurter concession in Long Island took a catastrophic dive the year after Dr. J left while frankfurter sales in Philadelphia rose spectacularly.

Return on investment as a standard for performance is also not as relevant for service and professional organizations or departments since the earning assets, human beings, are not on the balance sheet.

Accomplishment of incentive compensation purposes can be greatly facilitated in smaller firms by breaking them up into their component parts and assigning to each manager the assets and related income and expenses that he controls. For example, in an equipment distribution business one department sells new equipment and a second department sells used equipment, a parts division is responsible for maintaining proper inventory and service to customers, and a service department derives its major income from mechanics' labor. The incentives established for each department should be tied to the assets from which the departmental income flows and paid in accordance with the skill with which the asset is used.

But due caution must be exercised at this point as well. Be realistic about what you are paying for; remember that skill cannot be measured simply in dollar *amounts*. For example, the investment required for the sale of new and used equipment and inventory is substantial, and the contribution to profits from each sale made is potentially great. On the other hand, the investment in hard assets in the service department is not very great, and the contribution to profit from each job done is small. The tendency, then is to pay larger incentives to sales than to service people. But if measures of incentive pay included the degree of skill exercised in employing assets and the quality of customer relations, then perhaps sales and service would be paid more evenly. Without a service department that cements the transaction, the foundation for the next sale will be on shaky ground. There is much more to employing people profitably than selling tangibles at a profit.

We must also watch for perversion of the return on investment concept when a manager has decided to leave the company after his annual bonus has been computed. If his only interest was to show short-term profits, as it might well be, he would forgo advertising, repairs, maintenance, and the granting of reasonable credits to customers for disputed items, and would discharge every employee unnecessary to an operation stripped down to its bare bones (which at first appears to show the business is being managed well). After his departure, the company would have to repair a great deal of damage. For this reason many companies that include return on investment (ROI) or return on assets (ROA) in their performance standards add minimum levels of service for inventory, handling of customers and complaints, research and development programs, and capital investment.

The company comes first in setting up an ROI/ROA bonus plan. Profit is a necessity not just to provide a return on investment to shareholders but to permit the company to survive the mistakes managers make, to grow, and to replace depreciated dollars with inflated ones. Peter Drucker has pointed out that profit is best regarded as a cost, one of those items that must be recovered before a true economic profit has been earned.

In working out what constitutes a fair return to the company, remain conscious of the fact that accounting results usually are overstated. Profits are too high because they reflect inadequate depreciation charges, and the investment or asset base is too low because it is computed on historical rather than on replacement costs. We cannot set out a standard ROI below which an incentive bonus should not be paid. Each industry and company is unique; even within the same company the minimum will be found to vary from time to time with changing corporate strategies and for different divisions.

The following discussion is based on our experience in many

different industries. The plans or principles described generally were accepted by the managers affected, both those granting the bonuses and those earning them, as reasonable in terms of company and their needs.

Some companies, instead of concentrating bonus payments in a few key executives, have paid excess earnings to everyone and achieved spectacular results. The owners' philosophy is that the contribution of everyone in smaller companies is required in order to be profitable. If base salary levels are competitive and reflect differences in responsibility, an incentive pay system is fair if it first provides for the company and then distributes the excess profit to employees largely proportionate to their salaries.

Example. A small electronics manufacturer with 120 employees was owned by two engineers who had a simple bonus arrangement. After paying competitive salaries to all employees and themselves, they excluded from the pretax income subject to bonus 20 percent of the net worth of the company at the beginning of the year. This 20 percent was reserved for the company's needs and as a partial return to the two owners for their risk. *All* pretax profits in excess of 20 percent were distributed semiannually to all employees in proportion to salaries. Annually, the bonuses were 30 to 40 percent of the competitively set base salaries.

The motivational effects of this program were spectacular. Long before energy was a public issue, the workers set the thermostat at 65°F., concluding there would be greater profits if they conserved fuel. In every work group, people shared knowledge on how to do jobs so that when someone was ill or on vacation the work could be done without hiring part-time people. People who had observed the company would exaggerate how costs were controlled—they said that no paper clip had ever reached the floor falling from a desk because some hand caught it first. Although substantial social pressures were created through this group incentive pay, the company had practically no turnover, and the high wages and extremely high morale created a long waiting line at the employment office.

A short bonus summary:

1. Be flexible—there is no one right way. Sophisticated, sensitive companies are constantly reviewing their incentive plans.

2. Be pragmatic—we don't really know and can only guess what the influence of organization is on individual behavior. Experiment and use what works with your people and your company.

3. Create the opportunities for your participants to get major rewards—make it worth their effort to get rich.

4. Include measurability among the objective evaluation factors—if an objective cannot be measured, its appropriateness should be questioned. If it passes examination it should then be tied to the company goals and given a priority.

When incentive bonuses have been earned, some companies feel it helps retain managers to spread payment of the bonus over several years. For example, a manager earning a $60,000 salary receives a $20,000 bonus which is paid over five years only if he remains with the company. At that rate it will take him five years, assuming he earns the same bonus every year, before he receives the full $20,000.

There is little to be said for such an arrangement. The program implies that the manager is an $80,000-a-year man but not worthy of receiving the total amount at one time. If such an executive is offered $70,000 or $80,000 base salary by a competitor, the odds are that he will leave the company to satisfy his perception of his own economic worth. Bonuses serve their purpose best when subject to the least managerial discretion and should be paid as soon as possible after earned.

Improved variations of these retention techniques include the following:

1. The company grants a restricted stock option to which the executive gets substantial clear title (50–80 percent) if he remains for three to five years. The company's earnings must reach certain levels for the executive to earn the rest of the shares.

2. One-quarter to one-third of the bonus is based on one-year performance. The balance depends on a three- to four-year cumulative corporate performance, payable at the end of the period.

How Much Bonus for Superior Performance?

If you use compensation to get a person to change his behavior and improve his performance in the company's interest, he must see the increase or bonus he can get as significant. The increase must differ sufficiently from ordinary pay so that it stands a good chance of becoming a positive motivational force. Bonus payments of 10 or 15 percent have limited value. The limits, if there are to be any, should be high—up to 50 percent of a competitive base pay. When tied to profits, there should be no limit. If the potential for performance has no limit, neither should the incentive payments. Adopting a policy calling for such increases will, of course, result in a broader salary range and bonus than most companies are accustomed to. Raises of 20 to 30 percent are needed for exceptional performance.

Since bonuses should be used to stimulate and pay for extra performance only, they should come out of extra profits. To point managers' efforts in the right direction the bonus should be based on a performance formula known in advance to the participants. The formula used must first take into consideration the company's financial needs and a fair return to the stockholders.

Example. The pretax profit on the first 20 or 30 percent of the net worth at the beginning of each year is set aside for the stockholders and the bulk of the remainder is distributed without limit to key employees on an increasing percentage of pretax profits. The arrangement protects the corporation and affords the managers a chance (gives them incentive) to earn dramatically large bonuses, but only when the company is profitable.

Participants in a bonus plan must be carefully selected. Two practices are common: Put everyone in the bonus plan, or give a bonus only to those who create profits. Which practice is better is indicated by the fact that bonuses given independent of profits have little motivational value, particularly when given regularly and seasonally, as at Christmas time. They become an indistinguishable part of the expected total pay package; their only influence is a negative one when they are not given. It is better to identify who makes the key profit decisions and to distribute the bonus dollars proportionately.

SECRECY VS. OPENNESS

Some deep thinking is required on whether compensation is to be treated openly or confidentially. Merits and problems attach to both approaches and what is good for one firm can be destructive to another.

When there is secrecy about salary levels and the reasons for giving raises and bonuses, those administering pay do not have to explain their decisions, which can save a lot of time. On the other hand, being open about the reasons often turns up problems before they can mature to be destructive and produces information valuable to the refinement and advancement of the compensation plan. Moreover, secrecy is a sign of power if one withholds crucial information, and such power is not very often used wisely or for corporate-serving purposes.

Public disclosure of the pay levels and reasons for giving raises will probably reduce the importance of pay as a motivator if it is not tied to performance. When supervisors are unable to face their subordinates with proper explanations of the differences in pay relating to differences in performance, they avoid the personal problems by giving everyone the same raise or bonus or applying the same percentage.

Few companies are ready for total openness. It requires a high level of trust between people. We recommend that *levels* be made public, although we think it will be a long time before companies feel comfortable disclosing what individuals earn.

The question of openness and secrecy is tied strongly to management style. Compensation fits into a total management philosophy which usually is implied rather than explicit, felt rather than conceptualized. If management is otherwise open in its planning and about its plans, its admission of mistakes, and its desire to involve employees and get their ideas, then an open salary policy will be appropriate. However, if management decision making is centralized and close to the vest, if there are no known plans, and performance standards are lacking, then opening the door to public disclosure of salary levels will probably be a destructive act.

KEEPING COMPENSATION PATTERNS LOOSE

Compensation patterns should not stay fixed. Some recent currents were summarized in an article by John Perham.* Among the points that Perham made, amended for more current developments, were the following:

1. Even with the reduction in the capital gains tax more executives are choosing immediate cash compensation which they are willing to have taxed at the maximum 50 percent earned income

*John Perham, "The Changing Compensation Package," *Dun's Review*, September 1977. Reprinted with the special permission of *Dun's Review*. Copyright 1977, Dun & Bradstreet Publications Corporation.

rate. Options which once had special interest because of their tax advantage are almost dead.

2. The change in the tax law which reduced the maximum tax on income received through deferred compensation plans from 70 percent to 50 percent has obviously increased interest in those types of plans. Not only does the executive have a chance to accumulate money tax-free, but many programs are tying inflation, their own rate of interest, or their ROI into the amounts that have been put aside. Such a formula openly acknowledges inflation's erosion of the value of deferred compensation plans and the failure of the deferred amounts to earn even prime interest rates.

Comments on Turnover

In a society of executive shortage and social protection from starvation, fear is short-lived. Continued, it brings dullness and indifference. The threat of losing his job may cause a person to look at his employment fatalistically. If the ultimate motive for people to work is avoidance of the termination of their employment, if they know they are engaged in a contest which will result in only a few survivors, most people will lose interest because they know they cannot win.

Turnover rates should not be read raw. You should be more concerned with *who* leaves or does not (and why) than with sheer numbers. If any value is to be derived from turnover rates, it will be to see how compensation and other personnel policies may have affected the decision of those who stay and those who leave.

In one professional organization, a large number of the entrepreneurial top people left because they saw that there was no hope for them to be promoted within the next three years since the managers of the organization had made it explicit that they were top-heavy and did not want to aggravate the problem. The ones who left, of course, were those who had the best view of their worth with the most objectivity about their competencies. The firm now has a substantial gap between its top aging, competent managers and those who might be able to take over from them.

The Changing Nature of Key People

Those who are key people when a company is small usually continue to be considered key irrespective of their contribution as a company becomes larger. As a company grows, however, its skills and competence needs change; so should its compensation plans. In a growing company, compensation should be planned with the possibility that people will be brought in above the presently employed key people. A compensation plan attuned to a company of $5 million is not likely to be suited to a company doing $20 million.

A $20-million company is not a $5-million company expanded four times. A large rise in income and earnings is almost always accompanied by a disproportionate demand for expansion in the types and capacities of human resources required. At least part of the requirements are usually met by hiring professionals, people with specialized training and skills. That is another reason compensation planning must be kept ongoing and flexible.

Changes in size alone affect the mix of talents and the balance of job relationships needed to keep growth going. In companies with annual sales up to $10 million or so, it is possible for one manager to make all key decisions and keep things going through his personal effort. In such cases other managers are extensions of the boss; they are not expected to take initiative or challenge him, and their compensation is related to loyalty and longevity. In larger companies, however, the business begins to be overtaxed, which causes more errors than the firm's safety can tolerate.

When the pressures of size require a different breed of manager, the old compensation system has to be replaced with one that encourages risk and initiative or pays for identifiable division, brand, or staff results. Different needs and goals call for different measurements and different pay.

Evaluating Performance

To reward contribution to profits and to distribute rewards with equity, we must define who contributes to the company's earnings. This requires analysis of the functions performed within the company and evaluation of how well they are performed.

Example. Housewares company; annual sales of $10–$12 million; handles items that average 89¢ retail in a service relationship with large retailers. The key functions, which had a major impact on corporate profits, were analyzed as follows (not in priority order):

□ Obtain the customer: little turnover, long relationships with customers. This was a presidential task.

□ Choose and buy the merchandise.
□ Service the customers' outlets; supervise a field service staff of 30–45 low-salaried employees.
□ Deal with internal handling of low-value items: warehouse process orders, ship.
□ Deal with controlling, scorekeeping.

The following plan was proposed for incentive pay:

1. For each job establish three to five key result areas, participatively set. These results, as measurable as possible, would determine the priorities of the job. For example, for the internal handling job: items handled per man-hour, level of inventory, turnaround time for order handling.

2. If a manager achieved all his goals, he would receive 100 percent of his share of the bonus; proportionately less for less achievement, arranged and agreed to in advance.

3. A pretax ROI was established for company's growth and safety: 25 percent of net worth at the beginning of the year. Over the base, the formula called for increased percentages to be contributed to a bonus pool up to a maximum of 50 percent of base salary, later amended to 100 percent.

4. Of the total bonus pool, 75 percent was awarded on the basis of the formula and individual performance. The balance was discretionary for performance not anticipated in the standards.

Professional Firms

The problems of evaluation and wide ranges of earnings in a professional group trouble many people. They find it hard to agree on the measurements and feel that, since much of the judgment is subjective (which it is), the evaluation/profit-distribution process is divisive. An alternative is equal distribution of earnings after principals have been accepted into the firm as equals through exposure and testing.

Example. For the reasons mentioned above, this goal of equal earnings was proposed in a law firm where the range of partner earnings was $50,000–$250,000 (average $90,000). A consultant felt that the goal was unrealistic and also more destructive to the firm than the problems of evaluation and substantial difference in earnings. His reasons for this position were:

- □ In our society, money measures performance and relative status.
- □ The outstanding partners, on whom the firm's growth and success depended, would be the ones to give up earnings and position in the earnings hierarchy.
- □ The lower-level, less productive partners might feel slightly guilty about earning more than they would elsewhere, but probably would not be sufficiently unhappy to leave or initiate elimination of the equal pay system.
- □ The goal of equal earnings would require swallowing of differences, which could only harm the firm.

Following the consultant's recommendation the managing partner announced that they had decided to abandon the equality concept.

The case demonstrates a truth about all forms of planning: Plans can damage as well as help a firm. Compensation will damage an organization if it turns off or alienates those on whom the company depends. A good compensation program spotlights the extraordinary performer and satisfies the almost universal desire to be rewarded visibly and well for high productivity and contribution. A compensation program that disregards the power of extraordinary performers is almost guaranteed to fail.

A professional or service organization (law, accounting, distribution, insurance, computer programming, business service, and design firms) might analyze its key functions as follows:

Who brings in the clients, customers?
Who does the work?
Who maintains the professional quality and standards?
Who develops the staff?
Who administers, manages the organization?

To develop a compensation system based on these criteria requires agreement among the principals on:

What factors are important.
How to weigh each in relation to the others.
Ways to measure how they are being performed.

The measurements used should always have as few and distinguishable increments as possible, such as excellent, acceptable, not acceptable; or superior, average, inferior. We have never found it necessary to have more than a five-level scale.

In most professional or service groups, particularly those with low turnover among clients, a disproportionately higher value should be placed on obtaining the client-customer. In CPA firms, retention of clients may be as high as 98 percent. With insurance, janitorial service, business forms, linen supply, or exterminating services, the ratio can be 70 percent or higher. Thus, if the firm is concerned with both stability and growth, those bringing in the work should be rewarded more than those doing it. The only caution that needs to be exercised is to see that there is equal opportunity to bring in new clients or customers (so that some managers do not get locked into client or customer service).

Other measures are:

☐ The quantity of work done (billable or productive hours, number of dollars handled, number of people or crews handled).

☐ The technical skill available (determined by ranking people within the organization on this trait).

☐ The ability to develop staff (based on feedback from staff; observations of how people who work for individuals use their experience).

LONG-TERM CAPITAL ACCUMULATION

Compensation can be related to aspects of the firm other than immediate performance. A successful contractor used stock and cash as compensation to reward those who had helped build the firm, to increase the possibility that the firm would continue, and to create a market for his shares when he retired or died.

The company had a net worth of $2,400,000. The owner was in his early fifties with three children, none of whom was in the business although two might enter it. He decided not to wait until they decided what they wanted to do or were tested. He was more concerned with being fair to eight key people who had helped build the organization and who represented the best source of buying his stock when necessary.

The shares were priced at 60 percent of book value: a reasonable figure for the industry, in which future income was difficult to predict. Forty-nine percent of the shares were valued at $720,000. Assuming each of the eight employees received an equal number of shares over five years, the value of the stock distributed as compensation was $18,000 annually.

The major shareholder distributed unissued corporate (not his personal) shares in varying amounts based on his changing assessment of the contribution of the individuals and their likelihood of remaining and growing in the company. The $18,000 stock was ordinary income to the executives, who also received $18,000 in cash. The total of $36,000 required a tax of $18,000 (the purpose of giving cash). The result was that the employees received the stock at no cost to themselves. The corporation took a $36,000 deduction for each payment, saved $18,000 in tax, and thus had no cash cost for the stock distribution. Valuation was not a problem since there was no tax benefit to the company or the recipients if the value were higher or lower: Both were in the 50 percent bracket.

The program was designed to give recipients of the stock incentive to stay with the company so that they would be the market for the owner's shares when he retired or died. To employees who receive the bonus shares but do not stay the bonus ("gift," in truth) will be just that and no more.

To reduce the probability of having good employees leave, some companies first offer to sell shares to them, especially when top management knows the employees have the money to make the purchase. In other cases, the bonus shares are given without enough cash to pay the total tax. The employees therefore have to find the cash to pay part of the tax. The obligation can be satisfied from their regular cash bonus (assuming there is one) or out of their personal funds.

It is not possible, of course, to get a truly binding commitment from the recipients of the bonus stock to stay and work to redeem the shares of the older stockholders—at least not since the Emancipation Proclamation of 1863. Therefore, top management must test the willingness to accept the potential responsibility in any reasonable way.

6

The Special
Problems of
Smaller Companies

IN this chapter the leading compensation problems of smaller firms will be examined. As we have said before, "There are substantive differences between small and large firms that are not confined to differences in scale."* The field of compensation is not excepted; small firms have problems there which are unique to them.

GROWTH DISPROPORTIONATE TO SIZE

One of the characteristics of growing companies is an insatiable need for cash. When a company's rate of growth in sales or capital requirements is greater than its return on investment, it develops cash shortages that either limit growth or create liquidity problems.

*Cohn and Lindberg, *Survival & Growth: Management Strategies for the Small Firm* (New York: AMACOM, 1974), p.1.

In the face of constant corporate cash needs, the argument to keep executive salaries low is persuasive. "Wait, ride with us, and you will benefit from the efforts and sacrifices we are all making."

However, the practicality of the strategy must be coupled with an understanding of the critical importance of the few key movers in a company and the need to keep them satisfied so that growth momentum will not be lost. Studies show that companies of all sizes are influenced by the efforts of no more than five people, in many cases one to three.* This cadre of entrepreneurs has the intellectual resources and needs for achievement to take the risks involved in picking market niches and developing the competitively advantageous products and/or services to fill needs which are the sources of healthy growth.

The compensation plans for managerial "tigers" should not be the same as for maintainers, the administrators who support growth but do not initiate or produce it. The latter, when they are effective in their own right, need fair salaries, fringes, and some participation in profits, but they are more easily replaceable. The few key movers are not; certainly not within the time frames required for newcomers to learn the business, learn how the organization functions, and become leaders. One way to retain the "tigers" is to see that they do not need to invest time in being concerned with their compensation.

In most circumstances, that is not difficult to do. The amount of current cash required to keep the involvement of key people high is small in proportion to total cash needs. It is cheap money when courageously but carefully spent. Incentive bonuses between 40 and 100 percent of low base salaries can be dramatically motivating. Since they can be devised to come out of only incremental cash flow, they need not intensify the firm's cash problem. The compensation policy for the key executives of smaller companies growing fast should be base salaries at the low end of a competitive scale, a high corporate return (to satisfy corporate needs and emphasize the primacy of the financial interests of the company), followed by substantial participation by the few key people in the pretax profits earned over the basic corporate return. The arrangement costs nothing for average performance and little when high standards are exceeded.

Note the relationship between compensation policy and management style: If pay scales are in the middle of competitive ranges, the

---

*See Richard Normann, *Management for Growth* (New York: Wiley, 1977).

pay differences between performance levels small, and the rewards for longevity and loyalty high, you are probably attracting and retaining a high proportion of nonachievers. If the compensation program is designed to motivate achievers, you have better chances of attracting risk takers, who insist on being paid handsomely.

Achievers constitute approximately 10 percent of the managerial population. They gravitate to jobs and companies where they can set reasonable goals, enjoy the freedom to implement them, and control their activities through useful feedback. An essential element of feedback is the pay for reaching preset goals. The more substantial the pay the more effective the feedback. The bulk of the load in getting things done, maintaining the necessary structure to handle transactions and service customers, will fall on the shoulders of the nontigers.

That is not to say administrative skill is less needed than the other kind. One without the other is dangerous. Skilled administrators defuse crises by anticipating problems; they are problem solvers rather than problem creators (a necessary corollary to entrepreneurship) and therefore are less dramatic and visible. Without maintenance expertise the growth company descends into exciting chaos. Our point is that personnel in the two groups respond to different motives, and their compensation must therefore be different.

Finally, compensation programs for growing companies should aim at keeping key people satisfied as long as they produce. The other side of the picture is that the company will retain key people only as long as it continues to offer them the opportunity for professional and financial growth. Simply, an entrepreneur-minded organization and compensation policy may have a finite attraction for the manager who will rise with the company as long as the relationship has mutual benefit. When the learning rate starts running low and the chances of making substantial contributions and income are reduced, because the company's growth and profit opportunities have slowed down, the tiger may leave you. Say goodbye with thanks and let him go. You have both drawn as much as you can from his tenure. The lesson: Measure the value of retention in input-output terms for the organization and the individual. Always be prepared to accept the end of the relationship when the balance between the two is lost.

Example. Harry Dorner, marketing vice-president of a fast-growing distribution firm, had been the acknowledged stimulus for the company's move into new markets and the tripling of sales in his four years of employment. His salary had risen from $30,000 to $60,000. Looking ahead, Dorner saw little chance for his contribution over the next four years to equal that of the first four. Rates of sales and profit growth had slowed. With limited future professional growth and reduced financial rewards, he started looking for another job.

The president at first was upset when he learned of the vice-president's intention to leave. Upon reflection he realized that the company needed someone with skills different from Dorner's, able to consolidate and maintain what Dorner had created, and that the company had gotten from him the bulk of what he would probably contribute. Also, Dorner's salary increase curve had to flatten and that would pose a morale problem.

When Dorner left the company, the president's goodbye was gracious and thankful but also said with an understanding that the company now needed different skills.

FAMILY PROBLEMS

Pay given family members often bears directly on company fortunes. What is paid to family members and the bases for paying it can greatly influence the productivity of key nonfamily employees. The message that comes through in the many cases where incompetent family members have been given substantial positions or disproportionate pay is that the owners obviously do not respect the company—so why should anyone else?

It is always hard to keep exceptional employees. They have a healthy view of themselves, know their worth, and are not inclined to put up with compensation irrationalities, nepotism, and privileges based purely on family membership. If a family member performs exceptionally, no one will resent his being paid well. Exceptional nonfamily employees will appreciate their value as well as anyone else. On the other hand, the best employees resent incompetence rewarded. Good people want an environment that reflects well on their own competence, however good their own pay may be. High pay to incompetent relatives violates this standard: Unrealistic pay for family members is ruinous to even the best compensation plans.

We have never seen a firm with top-notch, long-term employees in which family members received rewards disproportionate to their contribution. Where family incompetents receive high salaries for operating forklift trucks, opening the mail, and having three-hour lunches, one usually also finds a dearth of talent in the longer-term employees. In such firms the people with top talent who happen in usually are gone as soon as they have reaped the benefits they came for. Therefore, don't pay family members unless they are employed in meaningful work, are paid in accordance with their competence, and contribute significantly. There is absolutely no way to pay a relative for doing nothing without eroding the soundness of the firm. If a family member is a nonproducer (and is dependent for income on the firm), arrange to pay him away from the business. Standards of performance for family members should be devised according to a corporate plan, not to individual taste.

One key to paying family members with significant portions of equity who insist on working in the business is to shift the income basis from high salaries to earnings payout (dividends), building the value of their equity, or a combination of the two. That may cause them to reflect on the impact of their behavior on the business since the performance of the business will be more closely related to their financial futures.

The whole question of family titles, fringes, pay, and bonuses is subordinate to the question: What does the corporate model say on such matters for *everyone* in the firm and, therefore, for family members? No effective compensation plan can distribute goodies independent of performance. Since exceptional people are also proud people, the chances of keeping them as employees and on the ball are in direct proportion to the extent family members are treated as other employees.

Measuring Performance

How do the CEO and family members find out how they are doing? Outsiders may be the best source of answering that question. You can devise standards of performance, and do measuring with planning, goals, objectives, strategies, policies, MBO, and so on, but how many times can such a procedure survive attacks by even one family member? If the family doesn't want to be objectively scrutinized, don't bother attempting to measure performance at all and forget about using compensation as a reward for accomplishment!

Closely held companies will do better trying to be professional, not just trying to get away with everything they can.

Ownership, Management Competence, and Pay

What is the relationship between holding stock and having managerial competence? It is purely random, particularly as a company and its managers grow older and as the needs for new skills change.

Example. Two brothers each owned 20 percent of a $30-million-a-year manufacturing firm whose shares were traded on the American Stock Exchange. One brother earned $18,000 as a truck driver and received his fair share of the dividends, $80,000 a year. The other earned $150,000 as chairman of the board and also received $80,000 in dividends. In this case, the brothers had accepted the relative difference in their abilities and were each drawing salaries equal to their job responsibilities. A clear line had been drawn between ownership and managerial competence.

In another case, an uncle of the controlling family occupied the position of warehouse manager but was only a good counterman. Because he was a relative, members of the family felt uncomfortable assigning him to anything but a managerial role. He caused inefficiencies, disrespect for management, economic loss, and was personally frustrated by the job. Finally, when a young member of the family, who was interested primarily in effectiveness, raised the issue of the uncle's position and pay, the belling of the cat was assigned to the young upstart. He sat down with his uncle and resolved the problem: The uncle would become a counterman and be given recognition for his knowledge of the product, but he would no longer be put in a position that he could not handle. His base pay would be reduced to his job level and the difference supplemented by after-tax gifts from other family members. Within a few years inflationary increases permitted elimination of the supplement.

To correct inequities in a family company, the practical answer is usually to leave salaries where they are for the incompetent members and raise those who require a difference in their pay because of a difference in their performance. But sometimes the solution lies in hiring outside managerial help. For example, a new company founded by two brothers was so small that each of them was able to draw only around $15,000 in salary. The advisory committee urged them to hire a marketing manager at $20,000—an unheard-of heresy in that a nonstockholder could be earning more than the two owners. Finally convinced that hiring the marketing manager was the only way the company could move off its low-level volume and exploit its good ideas, the two brothers did so. Within six years, sales had gone up by a factor of 15 and the after-tax profits were greater than the annual sales at the time they hired the marketing manager.

Another family problem was less easily dealt with. Two brothers each owned half of a service company. One handled all executive responsibilities. The other was lazy and irresponsible but refused to let his brother take more salary or benefits than he. His argument was simple: "I own half and want half. Pay is related to ownership and you're stuck with the bad deal our father left in his will." The competent brother has wrestled unsuccessfully with alternatives: liquidation, starting another company, the price of a fair salary differential, and has remained unhappily in the deadlocked situation.

Another case of a family-run company in difficulties is the Panther Company. A market leader in its industry, it has grown fast in the last five years under the leadership of its president, one of two cousins each of whom owns 50 percent of the company's stock. The other cousin heads the engineering department and is less interested in management responsibilities. Sales were $15 million and increasing 30 percent annually. Profits have been extraordinary: after substantial salaries and bonuses to the two cousins, 40 percent return on net worth at the beginning of the year. Historically, the cousins had been paid exactly the same. Bonuses were paid on an old formula that started with the first profit dollar and had no limit.

The company's management compensation program below the owner's level was also traditional; it contained no standards or explanation of what performance was wanted; raises and bonuses were totally discretionary and had become so routine and unresponsive to changes in annual profits that they were considered part of salary. Financial results were kept secret from the managers, but they were able to estimate the changing levels of operations from obvious physical evidence—number of people hired, pounds of shipments, overtime, plant and equipment expansion.

Solutions to these deficiencies were also routine: (1) establish individual standards of performance (many of the jobs had key measurable items), (2) develop a group incentive program tied to corporate profits in excess of a high ROI base, and (3) separate significant performance results with significant compensation rewards. The managers were unsophisticated and even after explanation of possible noncash rewards were interested only in immediate cash.

Before we turn to the more difficult problem of separating the performance and pay of the two cousin-owners, one element of the semiannual bonus arrangement is worth mentioning because of its general application.

Overall, pay was not a problem in Panther. The managers felt their pay, which was base pay *plus* the two semiannual bonuses, was reasonable. About half the people stated they lived only on their base salaries while the others lived on the total annual payments and felt their jobs were properly paid only when the total payments were considered.

The regularity of the two bonus payments, their almost mathematical and predictable increase, and their irrelevancy to corporate profits and specific performance changes reduced or eliminated the bonuses as a motivational tool.

The Panther pay system was not effective except as it kept people quiet and retained the present executives. Although most managers had set standards for themselves, they did not have clear agreement as to specific goals, priorities, qualitative measures, and the reward, if any, for achievement.

Each manager was asked to propose no more than a half dozen standards by which he could be measured; the owners would review and then negotiate the standards of a superior, acceptable, and unacceptable performance for each result. We then suggested that the two owner-managers set up regular annual appraisal sessions with each manager to discuss performance.

The bonus payment system had become more a means of deferring the paying of cash (since it was disbursed semiannually) than of rewarding people for their contribution or sharing in the company's profits. Here is how the bonus system was changed:

The total amount of present pay (salary and bonus) was frozen into an annual salary, of which 90 percent was paid currently. The two routine bonuses were eliminated. The remaining 10 percent of the total annual pay was left to the discretion of the individual manager, who was given a choice of the following items, all computed at their after-tax cost to the company:

- Cash (the remaining part of his new salary).
- Time off (computed by taking his 100 percent figure and dividing it by the normal work-year days to give a daily salary cost). As long as his job performance was not affected, the manager could choose to take additional days off equal to those computed.
- Certain fringe benefits, such as individual life insurance, through the firm's group policy. The additional premiums would be considered the same as salary, but the manager would be able to carry additional insurance and pay only the tax on the premiums in excess of $50,000 coverage.

A corporate bonus pool was set up for the managers below the top level. (In addition to the two cousins the top level included the chief marketing executive, whose contribution to the company everyone considered crucial.) The bonus pool was related to the pretax profits in excess of 30 percent of the opening net worth and was computed by contributing 2.5 percent of the salaries eligible for the bonus for every 1 percent over 30 percent earned up to the maximum of 40 percent of base salary. One-half of the bonus was set aside for achieving individual key results. The other half was paid if corporate profits exceeded the minimum. If a manager hit all his targets he was eligible for one-half of his bonus, 20 percent of his salary. Since these results were largely measurable and were agreed to in advance, few arguments over standards of performance were experienced.

Breaking the equality of the payments to the two cousins was more difficult. A measure of objectivity was achieved by including the key nonfamily marketing executive. Using the ranking procedure and independent evaluations of the contributions of the top three people, the bonus was allocated 50 percent to the cousin who was president, 20 percent to the marketing executive, and 30 percent to the engineering cousin. The same 30 percent pretax profit was used as a base, and 20 percent of the excess was set aside for the top executive bonus pool. To stay within the limits of reasonableness, a limit of 100 percent of base salaries was set for the next three years.

Base salaries were to be adjusted upward in line with executives in companies of similar size. A small differential separated the two base salaries to reflect the difference in jobs of the cousins. Because Panther's growth and ROI were above those of companies whose data were available, the figures chosen from salary surveys were the upper quartile and not the medians. Routine adjustments were anticipated for increasing the base for changes in the cost of living and sales volume.

In almost all cases, the attempt to equate ownership with salary or return on investment has been a catastrophe. It does not serve the purpose of keeping peace and also effectively demotivates the only family members who count—those who are able to contribute to profits of the company. What are the alternatives available to a family in these situations?

1. Isolate or insulate the incompetent person. That first requires an objective evaluation of each person's position and contribution. If it is considered unpolitic or impractical to terminate the employment of a family member, at least let him work where he cannot damage anyone's or the company's interests, and let him earn an amount proportionate to *his* contribution.

There is no law that says a family member must be an executive. Many do not want the responsibility. But economic realities say not to keep unproductive employees, whoever they may be.

2. Divide the business so that each member of the family takes responsibility for managing a proportionate share of the net worth. The competent ones can then do what they want, while the others will either fall by the wayside or, if wisdom strikes them, hire competent managers to handle their assets for them.

Example. Two brothers-in-law shared the ownership of five supermarkets and a small shopping center. They did not get along, in part because the younger man was so obviously more competent than his brother-in-law. Family problems had arisen because of disproportionate responsibility and contribution and equal compensation. The answer was to divide the six properties to satisfy their equity interests. Each retained the ownership and management of a significant piece and was freed of the other's managerial involvement.

3. If you can afford it, buy out the inactive or incompetent family member. From the conventional viewpoint, this alternative may appear to be a form either of slow suicide or a semiliquidation. But, calmy viewed, it seldom is. If the amounts involved in the buy-out can be stretched long enough and the payments equated with the net after-tax savings in salaries and benefits of the terminated stockholder-employee, the company may be able to support such a

redemption. Many managers are pleasantly surprised at the results of a discounted-cash-flow analysis of payments using as a rate of return the company's own historic ROI.

Example. After disputing for years over salaries, titles, fringe benefits, and how to run the business, three related shareholders, each owning one-third of a $5-million-a-year manufacturing firm, decided that one had to be bought out. The company's net worth was $600,000 and its earnings showed about a 10 percent ROI, equal to the industry average. A price of $200,000 book value was finally negotiated and was accepted by the two remaining shareholders and their families only after the present value of the payments was computed. Terms were ten years with interest at 6 percent on the unpaid balance.

Because of the power of present value computation (Table 2), the $230,000 after-tax payout shrank to about $144,000. Less salary, fringe benefit, and inflation savings, the deal was extremely attractive.

A major assumption behind this approach is that the cash retained, not used to pay the obligation, will be invested in the

Table 2. Present value computation.

Year	Principal	Payments After-Tax Interest Cost	Total	Present Value Factors @ 10%*	Present Value of Payments
1	$20,000	$ 5,700	$ 25,700	.91	$ 23,387
2	20,000	5,100	25,100	.83	20,833
3	20,000	4,500	24,500	.75	18,375
4	20,000	3,900	23,900	.68	16,252
5	20,000	3,300	23,300	.62	14,446
6	20,000	2,700	22,700	.56	12,712
7	20,000	2,100	22,100	.51	11,271
8	20,000	1,500	21,500	.47	10,105
9	20,000	900	20,900	.42	8,778
10	20,000	300	20,300	.38	7,714
Totals	$200,000	$30,000	$230,000		$143,873

*The present value concept relates to the value today of $1.00 in the future if you can invest at 10 percent. If you had $.91 today you would be in the same position as if you had $1.00 in a year—because $.91 invested at 10 percent for a year would yield 9¢, which added to the 91¢ equals $1.00. The computations deal only in after-tax cash flows.

business and on the average will earn 10 percent. That assumption, of course, is not always coupled with the buy-out decision, which is why so few family situations are resolved along these lines.

If you have a potential buy-out situation, stretch out the payments as long as possible, negotiate some part of the price as a deductible covenant not to compete, keep the interest rate low, and the buy-out is likely to be a partial solution to a family compensation or management deadlock.

An important consideration is the freeing of emotional, psychic energies which often become bottled up in the middle of a family compensation argument. Release of these energies back to the business may be the biggest savings of all. In one case, no one handled any business decisions except crises for six months while family executives fought over the price of a stock redemption. In another, resentment over the shady actions of a deceased relative was resolved only when his heirs were bought out. Meanwhile, a whole level of nonfamily management quit in disgust.

4. Recapitalize the business, giving the inactive or retired family members preferred stock and, for inflation protection, perhaps a small share of the common stock having no veto or a vote only when the preferred dividends are not paid. By freezing the interest of inactive members in preferred stock, the active members will be able to realize the benefits of their efforts in the increasing equity of their common stock. The shoals of changing tax laws have to be watched before undertaking preferred stock recapitalization, so check with your tax advisers. But recapitalization is one of the good answers to family compensation problems.

THE CEO'S PAY AND PAY LEVELS

In almost all companies, pay scales relate to the amount paid the top officer. Attacks by the IRS on unreasonable salaries (the CEO is the most visible) and the ability to take funds out of the company in fringe benefits and other tax-deductible ways have caused top salaries to rise more slowly in many smaller companies than those who are below the CEO would like to see. Our opinion is that the CEO salary should usually be the highest in a company but that the *total* compensation of an effective CEO need not always be the highest.

Among the ways in which executive pay is being changed in

response to the salary compression is to pay overtime to executives who have to put in substantial amounts for extended periods. Traditionally, a professional or a manager is supposed to work as many hours as his job requires. However, disproportionate effort may have to be recognized when the rewards are limited by constraints such as the CEO's salary. One technique is to provide overtime pay for work in excess of a certain number of hours (for example, 45 or 50 weekly) for an extended period of time (four or six weeks). We are sensitive to the fact that it is output rather than input for which one should pay. However, there are some jobs which, because of crises or seasonal work patterns, sometimes require much greater effort for the same output than other jobs. Employees putting out such efforts should be compensated for them.

If your pay levels are tight, consider rewarding the special performer by promotion. The tactic has its problems; it may require the addition of new pay levels (which does not relieve the problem of compression), and it will permit people producing extraordinary results to jump over some with more years with the company. But it will help keep the good performer happy. Furthermore, a person moving into a new level will have a greater range of salary growth because he normally will start at the bottom of the new level.

Another technique is to pay bonuses for special performance. To separate the one-time performance with one-time pay, do not build it into the base. It is smarter to give a bonus, even a discretionary bonus, for solving a problem or handling an especially difficult situation successfully than to add to base salary.

THE VALUE OF EXPERIENCE

In the absence of an evaluation system, don't exaggerate the value of experience, including your own. Never pay only for experience! Experience has value only in the results it produces, and that is what should be paid for.

Glenn Bassett of the General Electric Company has been concerned with the value of experience from the viewpoint of both the employer and the manager. He feels that in a period of two to five years most people give to a job 80 percent of what they are capable of giving during their normal working lives in that job, and in the same period they learn from that job 80 percent of what it is capable of teaching them.

One of the authors had the same managerial position for a dozen years. Looking back on what he learned and what the organization gained from his incumbency, he realized that he learned almost all that the job had taught him in the first five of the twelve years. In the last seven years so much of what he did was repetitive that he grew only slightly more as a manager. The assessment was confirmed from the viewpoint of the organization. His challenging, novel, change-producing ideas were largely contributed in the first five years. Much of the last seven years were spent defending his ideas and the changes they had caused against the attacks of other managers.

To employ personnel fully, their acquisition of experience must be managed. If we see that a manager is exposed to the things that he needs to develop and move ahead, we will have given him the experience he and the company will benefit most from. The lesson? Use the acquisition of experience as a compensation element (that is, pay for its acquisition) only in the first half-dozen years of job tenure. After that, forget it.

Instead of letting experience and growth happen randomly, work backward from a listing of those things that a competent manager should have done—not seen, not assisted at, not studied, not read about, but *actually performed*. If the number of repetitive experiences is reduced to the minimum necessary to satisfy two requirements, we will usually find that most people spend more time in a position than is needed for their and the organization's growth. The two requirements: Learn enough about a job so that those working in it full-time will not inadvertently or deliberately bamboozle you; learn enough so that you can move to a higher-level experience.

Looked at this way, experience has more specific and limited dollar value and its place in the compensation scheme may be clearer, but like discounted cash flow (DCF)—a declining value as time goes on—in a given job the content of original experience goes down with time.

ASSURING CORPORATE-SERVING DECISIONS

Decision making in smaller companies is naturally more susceptible to the affliction of selfishness, short-sightedness, and ignorance than in larger companies. Smaller firms are more easily dominated by one person, operate on smaller scales and in smaller markets, and have less diversity of experience and knowledge in their staffs—all of which translates into a smaller base for decision making and greater tendencies toward subjectivism.

To achieve its ultimate ends, compensation must operate in an environment in which decisions are primarily oriented to the corporate benefit. (There is no danger to the human factor when that is the case; no business can stay healthy if it does not care for its human resources.) A number of steps, including compensation planning, can be taken in that direction.

Healthy smaller companies recognize their limitations on the quality of decision making and take steps to broaden contacts with their environment. They raise their capacities to anticipate problems and deal with them by setting up a frame of reference for decision making at the top, a framework that can protect the firm from the erosions of arbitrary, uninformed, or self-serving decision making. The technique is to create an independent board of directors or an advisory committee comprising three to five outsiders in addition to inside members. The group meets at least quarterly (and, usually, also as called) with a carefully constructed agenda and serves in the following ways:

- As an open forum at which problems and ideas can be productively discussed, including compensation.
- As a means of restraining the chief executive or a dominant group from going to damaging extremes.
- As a group to which the closely held company owner-manager is accountable so that his own major decisions can be double-checked and his performance monitored and properly re-warded.

DEALING WITH LONGEVITY AND THE LONG-TERM NONPERFORMER

We think that the value of tenure is greatly exaggerated and that long tenure may even be dangerous to smaller firms. When we look at turnover statistics for small companies, we are impressed by the low turnover at the higher levels of management and the high rate of turnover at the lower levels.

In smaller closely held companies, it is common to find owner-managers who took power in their late twenties or early thirties, and who 30 or 40 years later are still running the company with the same group of obedient, dependent subordinates they inherited or surrounded themselves with. High base salaries are a common way of retaining such employees.

The protection of employees who are no longer growing and who no longer contribute to the company's growth is a special characteristic of the paternalistic closely held organization. The value of executives in smaller firms is usually measured by the wrong benchmarks, such as long years of service, long hours, contentment with pay, and deference to the privileges of ownership. As long as the goals of the enterprise remain low-keyed and unambitious, there are few problems, but when a firm begins to aim at exploiting its opportunities, trouble then follows. When a manager who has lost the ability to contribute at a key level reaches job and compensation levels that are high in relation to those of other managers, the productivity or retention of those still contributing become problems. Top management that wants to move the firm ahead has to decide what to do with old Charlie or face the certainty that he will stand in the way of realizing improved results.

There is no pleasant answer to the problem, but the right answer from the compensation planning viewpoint is to put the company's needs first and then handle the obsolete employee in a style which fits the company's personnel and management philosophy. Because of its high emotional content, the visibility of the decision, and the loud message sent to other employees on the treatment of those who have run out of steam, the problem merits thoughtful action.

The right answer often is to move the employee down or sideways in the organization to a position he can handle, and to adjust his salary immediately for the change in job. If the difference between what he is and should be earning is tolerable, leave the old salary base alone and give no raises until inflation catches up.

When the spread between the employee's pay and that deserved by the job is significant, the employee should be given the option of taking pay appropriate to the job or of leaving. Note the choice—*he* has the option. Our experience is that he will generally accept the lower-level position *if* he can do so with face-saving grace. Whether that is possible is more a function of the approach top management takes than the employee's strength of personality and his need for retaining a job.

At least two reasons can be found for a manager who fails in a position to which he has been appointed: He handled the job poorly because of personal weakness or inadequacies; or, because he lacked skills or experience, the job was wrong for him and someone made a mistake in transferring him to it. If top management can admit openly or by implication that the failure to achieve expected performance stemmed from its mistake in assigning the person to the job, and if it finds a more appropriate position for him, the long-term demoted employee can bear more easily the reduction in status and pay and the pain of failure.

In our experience over 90 percent of employees who are given the chance to stay at a lower-level job that they can handle will do so after being demoted in position and pay—if the atmosphere is not accusatory. Failure on the job is rarely a surprise—the employee knows he has not met expectations and is often relieved to be reassigned. As in other personnel and compensation policies, the handling of failure is one of the visible signs of management's ethical values.

If termination is the only practical answer to a long-time employee, many companies acknowledge their responsibility by providing separation pay that helps bridge the gap between available jobs and the last level.

REASONABLE COMPENSATION

Executives of closely held companies are particularly vulnerable to IRS challenges of whether or not their compensation is "reasonable." The exposure to double taxation (the corporation and the individual) on the disallowance of compensation makes it crucial that pay be considered reasonable. Although "an attempt to give a specific meaning to the word 'reasonable' is trying to count what is not number and measure what is not space," from as early as 1918, the Treasury Department regulations have provided that "the test of deductibility in the case of compensation payments is whether they are reasonable and in fact payments purely for services."

From this and from a survey of recent tax court proceedings, we may divide the issue into two main areas: (1) *amount*—whether the compensation payment is reasonable in relation to services performed, and (2) *purpose*—whether in fact the payment is made for the services rendered.

An example of this approach is the case of Charles McCandless vs. U.S. A father and son each owned 50 percent of the shares of the corporation. Earnings and officers' salaries were rising, but no dividends were being paid to the McCandlesses. The court found that the salaries paid were reasonable, but a portion of the salaries paid was disallowed on the premise that the absence of any dividends required that some part of the salaries be viewed as a distribution of earnings. The court determined that 15 percent of net income would be a reasonable return on equity capital, and held that proportion of the salaries to be nondeductible dividends. In this case the court used the company's dividend history as an important factor in determining reasonableness.

The issue that some part of even reasonable pay may be exposed to dividend attack has only recently been cleared up.

One possible defense against having to attribute a part of salaries to dividends even when the salaries are reasonable lies in the basic economics of smaller businesses. Large publicly held companies often pay no dividends, their directors choosing to reinvest their earnings in sales growth and market share. The payoff from this strategy is that increased rate of return, higher growth rate, and larger market penetration will eventually create a higher price for the stock. It is part of the irrationality of the tax laws that the owners of smaller companies that want to do the same sometimes get stuck with taxes the large companies do not. Further, companies that pay no dividends often pay their top executives, stockholders or not, far higher salaries and bonuses in order to keep them than the owners of smaller businesses can afford to pay themselves.

Growth requires outside sources of capital or reinvestment of earnings. Smaller companies have fewer and more demanding sources of credit than large companies. Their access to capital and long-term financing markets is limited. Retained earnings are the major capital source, and dividends reduce the cash available and the rate of growth.

Smaller companies, especially closely owned ones, have additional reasons for not paying dividends; they need to provide for the eventual redemption of their shares when stockholders leave the company to keep the stock from getting into the hands of undesirable parties, provide for the family needs of a deceased or departed shareholder (including payment of estate taxes), and by reacquiring Treasury stock, make it available to new, younger managers to secure their services. Those are valid business reasons not to pay dividends while paying large salaries—always, of course, subject to the reasonableness test.

Today most executives, whether they own stock or not, prefer cash as a reward for their performance. The decline in the use of stock options and other forms of stock ownership by publicly held companies is even greater among closely held companies where the market for minority shares is only within the company and is subject to severe limitations of options, price, and terms.

The exposure to dividend-payments taxation is much smaller in a company with limited capital whose success is based mainly on personal service. Engineering, medical, dental, accounting, computer service, insurance agency, or other firms that are dependent on the personal skills of their chief officers are less likely to be attacked for high salaries and nondistribution of earnings than those which require heavy capital investments.

What Is "Reasonable"?

In general, reasonableness is determined by comparing the amount of compensation paid to the value of the services performed. A corporation may not claim that sums paid to individuals are deductible merely because the value of a group's services in the aggregate accords with the amount paid. The determination is made on an individual basis and not in terms of aggregate compensation paid to all employees.

There are two tests of reasonableness: The individual's salary must be reasonable, and employees' salaries in total must be reasonable. Moreover, a company cannot take comfort from the fact that its compensation scheme is not highly original. In the words of one court, "each corporate tub must stand on its own bottom." Following is a list of factors which enter into a decision of reasonableness, compiled from numerous court cases:

Salary history of the individual. A sudden, major increase in the pay of an individual will draw the attention of an auditing agent.

Dividend history of the corporation. Dividends conspicuous by their absence in a background of corporate earnings will encourage an adverse finding on reasonableness.

Compensation scale for employees generally. Compensation is compared to that of companies of the same size in the area.

Salary scale of the industry. The regulations hold that "it is, in general, just to assume that reasonable and true compensation is only such amount as would ordinarily be paid for like services by like enterprises under like circumstances." This is probably the most significant factor in a reasonable compensation case.

If salary comparison with other companies cannot be done or is unfavorable, you should be able either to demonstrate that the employee's duties are more significant than those performed by a competitor, because they require unique skills or show high profitability, or to prove lack of comparability on other grounds.

Qualifications of the employee. A salary higher than could otherwise be justified may be reasonable if it can be established that the employee in question is exceptionally qualified or has rare skills.

Employee's contribution to the success of the business. In particular situations, the services of an individual may be indispensable to the continued prosperity of the business. If it can be demonstrated that the employee built up the business, controlled relations with major customers, or was responsible for its growth of profits, a large salary may be justified. This is often the case in incentive compensation agreements.

Formality and timing of corporate action. Formal board resolutions regarding the compensation for principal officers in closely held companies carry less weight than in large companies in preventing courts from substituting their judgments for the directors'. Nonetheless, such resolutions should not be ignored. The absence of a formal corporate approval of salary arrangements in a closely held company may be grounds for disallowing compensation deductions.

Timing is important: If a compensation plan is formulated at the end of the year after the profit picture emerges, the presence of a profit-distribution motive may be more conspicuous. Compensation decisions should be made at the beginning of the year and earnings made contingent on year-end results (which is good planning anyway). In this way, they are an incentive to performance rather than a distribution of profits already accumulated.

The essential problem is to demonstrate an acceptable business or economic reason for compensation other than mere avoidance of taxes.

What the IRS Looks At

Two factors that invite IRS investigation and disallowance appear in the regulations themselves: (1) compensation payments which bear a close relationship to the stockholdings of officers and employees, and (2) contingent compensation, where the payments are not dependent on future events, especially pretax income.

There are other factors which may lead to disallowance. A review of court cases reveals that your vulnerability to disallowance increases the more the factors are present. However, the amount of compensation considered reasonable will always depend on the specific case.

The following factors may attract IRS attention:

☐ Absence of dividends or a small payout in relation to earnings.
☐ Bonuses paid in proportion to stockholdings.
☐ A record of negligible or no taxable earnings (which have been wiped out through high executive salaries or bonuses).
☐ Bonus payments established *after* the profit picture for the year is apparent.
☐ A large increase in compensation compared to the previous year (a large decrease also may attract attention to previous years' compensation).
☐ Compensation paid to relatives of stockholders.
☐ Absentee management.
☐ Payments to stockholder-employees out of proportion to payments to nonstockholders.

Other forms of compensation that relate to IRS decisions are: deferred compensation; pension plan contributions; stock options; and payments for traveling and entertaining expenses, medical expenses, life insurance, or other fringe benefits. In the case of these forms of compensation, even though the amounts may be deemed "reasonable," they may be disallowed as a deduction unless clearly intended as compensation for services rendered.

The original intent of payments to executives will also be

considered in determining whether they are compensation. For example, unrepaid advances that the IRS claimed were constructive dividends could not be considered compensation since the corporation had not treated them as compensation (it excluded them from W-2 form) and the employee had not picked up the amount as salary.

The same situation exists with travel and entertainment expenses that are subsequently disallowed: They cannot on hindsight be called compensation. Other payments which are nondeductible are amounts paid as bribes or to exert political influence.

Any deduction may require detailed substantiation. If your company uses any of the above forms of payment except cash, discuss the details with a tax or compensation adviser. For example, compensation to executives can be in corporate stock. If fair market values are used, the normally positive tax consequences will be protected.

Comparisons

Comparison with compensation paid in other companies is good but should never be made the sole basis of compensation. It violates the principle of primacy of corporate interests. On at least one score they are objective. At the most they can tell you what you ought to be paying your people when you are below scale; at the least they can tell you where you have to start in being more creative with pay than your competitors. In addition to the normal sources of industry and association figures, noncompeting colleagues may be able to supply you with salary information.

The test of comparative earnings can be applied in several ways: to absolute amounts, to percentages of executive salaries to sales, and also to the incentive formulas. Many unique smaller companies, serving special markets and with few competitors, cannot easily get comparative information. They should seek salary data for industries that serve the same *markets* but with different products. The number of specific sources for a small item may be few, but the number of vendors serving the same field may be large.

Where specific comparisons can be made and they are unfavorable to the desired level of compensation, consider compensating the executive in accordance with the level of skills or economic control he exercises. Typical examples include royalty payments for inventions or engineering improvements and sales commissions for developing or handling key accounts. The payments are in addition to the compensation paid for general administrative duties.

Compensation for Services Rendered in Previous Years

Compensation paid in the current year for past services may be deducted even though the amount is in excess of reasonable compensation for the current year's services. The payments can go back quite far; in one recorded case they went back 13½ years.

But to avoid disallowance, compensation for past services should clearly be so designated. Of course, compensation in subsequent years will be lower unless other justifications for higher payment occur.

Since deductions are allowed only for services "actually rendered," total absence of services or payment in respect of services to be rendered in the future are not deductible. When someone is paid but is unable to work or if payment is represented for work to be done in the future, deductibility is dubious.

Bonuses and Contingent Compensation

Bonus payments are not treated separately in IRS considerations. They are allowed as deductions when they are paid in good faith as compensation for services actually rendered, but the total of salary plus bonus must not exceed the limits of reasonableness. Thus, timing—that is, when you pay a bonus for what—is an important factor in considering the deductibility of bonuses.

Contingency pay arrangements lead to variations in pay from one year to another. This is normal since they are, by definition, based on performance which is to take place in the future. The most common example is the incentive bonus computed on a percentage of pretax income. Reasonableness is tested not so much by the amount paid as by the background of the arrangement. The regulations provide that payments will be allowed as compensation if they are made at "arm's length," the circumstances taken into account being those that existed when the contract was *made*, not those that exist at the time of the investigation.

The absence of cases of reasonable compensation which involve dealings between truly unrelated individuals can be taken as evidence that the IRS tends to regard compensation arrangements made in closely held companies as under a cloud. An element of objectivity may be introduced if truly independent directors or an outside consultant sets the pay and the contingent incentive program before the results are known. A written report, backed by thorough homework, can be useful.

Contingency pay arrangements have given rise to two trends in the courts. One position is that contingent pay arrangements are not necessary for stockholder-officers because their stock ownership gives them sufficient incentive to improve the business. The Fifth Circuit Court, on the other hand, has taken a more liberal attitude: "The tax gatherers ought, in appropriate cases, to consider the fact that the sole stockholders often risk not only their capital and their credit but also the loss of their time and effort, knowing full well that the corporation must first earn their salaries before they can be paid and that the salaries of all other employees must be paid before theirs; and to that extent their salaries are more or less contingent. Generally, contingent compensation is expected to be larger than compensation that is fixed and definite." A lead from this position is to set stockholder-manager base pay competitively and, when the results justify, provide substantial bonuses. The risk factor is then highlighted.

An example of a spectacular contingent bonus plan which included most of the provisions for ensuring reasonable executive pay was that of the Jordan Construction Company. With a net worth of only $400,000 the company managed in one extraordinary year to earn $1.1 million pretax. The shares of the company were held by George Jordan and his second cousin, Fred Vincent. They did not get along, primarily because George felt that he was not properly compensated for obtaining the large contract which was the source of the profit and for his assuming responsibility for all the management functions. Each man took the same $60,000 salary and expense package.

To resolve the argument and to keep George from leaving the company, Fred agreed to the following program:

1. Bonuses totaling $100,000 were paid to six top managers and foremen, none of whom held stock.

2. Because the year's results were unusual, George and Fred declared a special dividend of $40,000.

3. An incentive bonus was created in the first quarter of the fiscal

year when it appeared the results would be special, but long before anyone had a firm idea of the actual income. It was based on one-half of the pretax profits in excess of 50 percent of the opening net worth and would be divided between the two shareholder-managers on the basis of the direct labor hours each supervised.

4. Base salaries would be changed to give George a differential over Fred of $10,000 a year up to a maximum of $40,000.

As a result of this program George received a bonus of $300,000, Fred one of $200,000, after the dividends and non-shareholder bonuses were paid. To date, the agreement has been accepted by the IRS.

Among the reasons for the acceptance of the program by Fred, George, and several outside consultants were the findings of informal research which showed that compensation paid to the two principals, especially George, was no more than that which the company would have had to pay to anyone who had brought in and managed a major contract. The decision to pay substantial bonuses to the other managers and to declare a dividend showed that the owners realized that the extraordinary profit created earnings beyond the company's current needs. The limit on the incentive bonus—after providing a reasonable return to the company—was one-half the pretax profit and indicated that the compensation program was concerned with protecting the company.

Situations Where Compensation Is Not Allowable

In general, according to the "ordinary and necessary" business expense requirements of the regulations, if an amount does not constitute an ordinary and necessary business expense, it is not deductible even though it is intended as compensation for services actually performed and paid for reasonably. A good example is an expenditure for the services of a domestic in the taxpayer's home. Even though the domestic is necessary to the working of the person reporting the expense, the salary is regarded as a personal expense and nondeductible.

Other examples are payments which are deemed reasonable in amount and intent but which fail as a deduction because they are capital expenditures (salaries for architectural services) rather than ordinary or necessary business expenses, or compensation for services on behalf of a related taxpayer, such as salaries paid by a corporation for services rendered on behalf of its wholly owned subsidiary.

Essential Steps to Avoid Attack on Reasonableness

We will conclude discussion of this subject with a list of steps to take to avoid having the reasonableness of compensation questioned. Since reasonableness is not a matter of black and white, the best advice in making compensation decisions is to be aware of the factors mentioned above and at the least on any important question to stay within a broad grey area.

1. When you have high earnings and the cash to pay at least a minimum dividend, do so. Conspicuous in its absence, the payment of a minimum dividend creates an aura of greyness. It is also generally harder for an examiner to say "pay more" rather than "pay some."

2. Avoid compensation, increases in compensation, and bonuses which appear to be based on stockholdings. Avoid large increases unless you can prove the need to catch up for previous unreasonably low levels.

3. Set salary and bonus formulas early in the year; that maximizes reasonableness because the situation at the date of setting the formulas is controlling, not the situation when the profit picture becomes clear.

Contingent arrangements enjoy more latitude than fixed amounts. However, to be effective, they must be bona fide, agreed upon by free bargaining, and stay within reasonable limits.

4. Utilize deferred and indirect methods of compensation. Fringe benefits tend to be questioned less than salaries and bonuses even though their economic effects may be the same.

Payback Arrangements in Case of Disallowance

To reduce the double tax impact of disallowed excessive compensation, some tax practitioners recommend that key executive-shareholders enter into agreements with their coporate employer to repay any disallowed amounts. This concept makes economic sense only when the executive is a substantial shareholder and would benefit from the repayment.

Following are the requirements which seem necessary to create a valid repayment agreement:

1. The board of directors passes a resolution or has the corporate by-laws require repayment of compensation found excessive by the IRS.

2. Put the by-law or resolution in effect in the year prior to the year of the possibly excessive compensation.

3. Have the executive sign the agreement or otherwise indicate his awareness of the obligation prior to receiving his compensation.

4. Be sure that state law permits enforcement of the resolution or by-law. Following is an example of a clause covering this point and includable in the executive's employment contract:

> If any part of the compensation paid to_____is disallowed by the IRS as a deductible expense to the company on the grounds that it is not reasonable compensation, and if this determination by the IRS is upheld after the company carries the issue to the Tax Court, or decides not to,_____agrees to reimburse the company for the disallowed amount within sixty days after the company has notified_____of the disallowed amount. If the company has not received the full amount due within sixty days of such notification, it shall withhold up to one-third of future compensation payments due_____until the amount owed the company has been fully paid.

The basis for the deductibility of the repayment is that it is a legal obligation with an unquestioned amount.

Summary

Unreasonable compensation which is disallowed may be subject to double tax payments: once by the recipient and once by the corporation. Moreover, the burden of proving reasonableness is on the corporation.

The first line of defense against the potentially costly attack on the reasonableness of compensation is to be prepared in advance by taking steps to create the appearance of reasonableness. The aforementioned methods are not suggested as means of tricking the IRS but rather ways by which one can avoid having reasonable compensation appear to be unreasonable.

7

Fringe Benefits

FRINGES are much more useful compensation tools than is generally appreciated. They are not only tax-saving but motivational devices. Smaller companies have great opportunities to make imaginative use of fringes because of their tax consequences, status implications, and motivational value, and because they have come to be an expected part of normal compensation. Purely in economic terms, fringes deserve attention. The cost of what are generally included as fringes rarely runs below 25 percent of base salary and can easily reach 50 percent. However, fringes should be of concern to smaller-company managers for more important reasons.

Fringes can affect performance, attract and retain managers, and separate levels of employees. Fringes have competitive uses; the smaller-company manager who understands where individual attention will pay off, where he has to be competitive to retain top producers, and what costs should be made variable has started to have an appreciation of the use of fringes.

IMPORTANCE OF ADDING FRINGE BENEFITS SLOWLY

Growing smaller companies should add fringe benefits slowly because they quickly become chiseled in granite; they are soon seen as part of normal pay rather than as extras. After providing the benefits required by competitive hiring and retention purposes, you will probably do better to delay adding additional benefits until you are confident they can be afforded and are not likely to be retracted in the future. The occasional exception is of gothic porportions; it is usually forced on a company by circumstances rather than by choice, as for example, when a retirement program (pension or profit-sharing plan) must be eliminated after a series of disastrous losing years because the continued cost may cause bankruptcy.

The elimination of fringes as punishment for inadequate performance is usually impractical. The rarity with which fringe benefits are dropped evidences that. Once an executive has earned a benefit, he expects to continue to enjoy it. There is no way to remove it without uproar except to terminate him or take it from all executives. Instead of taking from a nonperforming manager his club membership, reducing him to the use of a plebeian-size car, and cutting back on his medical reimbursement plan and extra life insurance, the wiser course would probably be to fire him.

There are other reasons for going slow in adding broad-gauge fringe benefits. As long as the earned income tax rate is limited to 50 percent, many managers want to spend their money their own way. They understand the economies of buying insurance coverages in groups, but they often choose cash and the freedom it offers over the company-paid fringe benefit.

Checklist of fringe benefits. Here is an outline of important fringe benefits that compensate executives in small companies today. Use it to select the benefits that are likely to motivate your top managers and to support your management goals and style. The list is divided into three categories (Necessities, Participation in Profits and Provision for Retirement, and Perquisites), depending on the function of the particular fringe benefit.

Because of changing tax rules, local IRS interpretations of regulations, and the exposure to double taxation on disallowed items, it is wise to check with your local professional tax adviser on the proper application of each of the following items to your company.

NECESSITIES

These include items of compensation such as basic medical and life insurance coverages, vacations, some retirement programs, and payment of professional dues and meetings—now so common they are expected as part of pay. Their absence creates a negative motivational effect but their presence does not necessarily create a positive motivational effect. The benefits you choose to give in this class should be selected to satisfy your management philosophy, but remember they will have little effect in attracting or changing the behavior of managers.

Medical, surgical, and major medical insurance. If you have enough employees to make the investigation worthwhile, obtain quotations from several carriers. If your group is sufficiently large, you may be able to get preferred rates. Clarify your philosophy: Do you want the company to pay for everything or only those expenses which are difficult or impossible for the average person to handle?

In the second form of coverage (the one we recommend), routine small items are excluded from coverage. The savings in omitting them are substantial since insurance company administrative costs relate more to the number of claims filed than to the size of the claims. Yet the protection against catastrophic illness or injury is not diminished.

Group life insurance coverage. The advantage here is that premiums for up to $50,000 term coverage are not taxable or includable in the income of the insured and are deductible. Many companies stop their thinking about group life insurance at the $50,000 level because of this tax provision despite the fact that many executives want or need additional coverage.

Consider offering more insurance, payable by the company. Managers will have to pick up as income the amounts related to the coverage over $50,000. This is usually less than the company's contribution, and is less onerous than paying the same premiums with their own after-tax dollars.

Other insurance coverage. Most small company managers, stockholders, and employees are underinsured. Check with your life insurance agent for a description and their tax consequences of the many types of programs aside from group coverage available for individuals. A popular example is ordinary life insurance, financed by the minimum-deposit plan, which permits part of the annual payments to be deducted as interest (after certain provisions are met).

Medical reimbursement plans. These have lost some of their attraction with the reduction, for payments received beginning after

1979, of the possibility of targeting the benefits to a select group of managers. Simply, the plan calls for the company to pay for the uninsured medical, dental, and drug expenses of employees and their families without requiring the reimbursements to be included as income by the employee who receives them.

For the payments to be tax-exempt, the program cannot discriminate in favor of stockholders or highly paid employees and must include 70 percent or more of all employees (more than three years' employment, over twenty-five years old, full-time, not covered by a union medical plan) or 80 percent of those eligible.

Put an annual limit on the amount the company will reimburse an employee—common figures are $1,500 to $5,000. Although IRS approval is not needed, determination letters will be available and in nonsensitive situations should probably be requested. Properly drawn corporate minutes should be on file.

If highly paid employees receive more reimbursement than others in a discriminatory way, the taxable portion is calculated by multiplying the total amount paid to the individual by a fraction—the numerator is the amount paid all highly paid managers under the plan; the denominator is the amount paid all employees in the plan.

Example. Assume all eligible employees receive $50,000 under the plan and highly paid employees receive $20,000 of that amount which was deemed discriminatory. If one of the highly paid employees received $4,000, his taxable portion would be $1,600: $4,000 times $20,000/$50,000, or 40 percent.

Key managers may still be ahead if they have to pick up as taxable income amounts deemed to be discriminatory. Further, the rules on discrimination relate to an *un*insured reimbursement plan. If the employer wants to pay the premium, he can buy individual medical insurance policies only for specific high-salary or key executives.

The savings are considerable. A manager with an adjusted gross income of $50,000 and in a 50 percent top tax bracket cannot deduct the first $1,500 (3 percent) of his medical costs not covered by an insurance program. The company's reimbursing him for these costs saves him $1,500. For costs over $1,500 that he might otherwise deduct, the reimbursement plan saves 50 percent, the share of the deduction that is his own money.

Medical examinations. The evidence is not clear, but there is probably enough support for the value of *executive physicals* to suggest that they be routine, company-paid benefits. By insisting that every executive in key jobs take an annual physical examination, the company implies that the manager's health is important. Practically, the examination may discover a correctable condition in time: Diabetes, prostate problems, and high blood pressure are among the more common conditions diagnosed. A further advantage is that executive physicals are not subject to the medical reimbursement limitations.

Long-term disability insurance. If a long waiting period is part of this type of policy, it offers protection at reasonable cost from the financial hazards of permanent or long-term disability. Managers over thirty-five are more likely to be disabled than to die during their normal working lives.* In small companies it is wise to have a disability salary plan to take care of this exposure and to back it up with a long-term insurance policy.

A common sick-leave salary plan provides for continuity of full salary for 3 to 12 months, followed by partial pay for an additional 6 to 12 months. The long-term insurance program fits into the corporate plan. Better to plan for the disability contingency (using corporate salary continuity for the first period and then insurance) rather than confront the difficult human problem of what support a disabled manager should receive *after* a disability has occurred.

Vacations. These are usually related to employment tenure. Although work habits and the anxieties resulting from work pressures are infinitely varied, there may be some value in offering extra vacation time to executives, in part to reward them for their position, and in part to increase the chance that longer or more frequent vacations will protect a valuable human asset. In some small companies where the centralization of authority and decision making has made it difficult to test younger managers, long vacations are aimed not only at getting the older manager away from his work for his sake, but also at forcing rotation of responsibility to younger people.

As managers move toward retirement, longer vacations may ease the older manager's transition to his new life. In one small company, every manager who reaches sixty is forced to take an extra month off for every additional working year. By the time a manager in that company reaches 65 he is working only half time, is gently being

---

* Edwin White and Herbert Clasman, *Business Insurance*, 4th ed. (Englewood Cliffs, N.J.: Prentice-Hall, 1974), pp. 421-422: "On the average one out of three persons now age thirty-five will suffer a long-term disability of at least three months before reaching age sixty-five, and the average length of such disability will be over five years."

forced to plan his life, and has been away from his job in long enough periods so that his potential successor(s) could be tested.

Travel and accident insurance—24-hour coverage. In connection with vacations we should mention full travel and accident coverage, a policy which fills a gap in travel coverage often forgotten by the manager and insures him at work, at home, and on vacation.

Professional dues, publications. It would be a rare management that did not want its executives to keep up to date in its industry or profession. There is general support for subscriptions and dues directly related to professional or trade organizations. Taste and imagination can be applied to this area if we expand the definition of what a manager should know. The higher the manager level the more he has to concentrate on the outside world and the partially unknown areas of competition and social, legislative, and economic changes likely to influence the business. Many companies urge their managers to read broadly and support the suggestion by paying for journals, magazines, and books of general interest which may expand the intellectual horizons of the firm.

Similarly, attendance at mind-expanding seminars and courses, beyond those promising immediate profit payoff, not only can help the firm in the long run but can create an atmosphere of intellectual ferment which may enhance the firm's professionalism.

In choosing subscriptions or seminars, remember that the expensive cost factor is scarce managerial time more than the out-of-pocket cost of publications or programs. To avoid dilettantism, apply a healthy dose of tough-minded skepticism and make this fringe benefit available only for special rewards.

In a consulting organization the managing partner did everything possible to make it a desirable norm that key personnel learn, expand their interests, and test ideas in new fields. He budgeted seminar and course attendance expenses (and insisted they be spent) because the firm's future depended on maintaining a flow of new ideas. The increase in professional quality was hard to measure but acknowledged. Further, the firm's technical reputation was enhanced and bright applicants sought it out.

PARTICIPATION IN PROFITS AND PROVISION FOR RETIREMENT

Included in this category are items related to power, status, and longevity. There is a wide choice of benefits available in this group, many of which can be designed for individual need and taste. Examples are a variety of retirement programs, incentive bonuses, profit participation plans, ownership of company stock, phantom stock, appreciation rights.

Profit-sharing and pension plans. Few companies in business for ten or more years are without a formal retirement plan. As a result, the motivational values that profit-sharing and pension plans once may have had have become lost in their widespread availability. People now expect the plans; lack of the plans is more a negative recruiting factor than anything else. They have low motivational value because the payoff is too far in the future to affect current behavior. Retirement plans avoid demeaning negotiations by older employees for retirement benefits; they are usually designed to yield the highest benefits to owner-managers by having payments keyed to salary and/or longevity.

Individualized retirement plans. Where the company cannot afford or chooses not to have a general retirement program for all employees, a smaller firm can design individual contracts with selected managers. Although the fulfillment of most tailor-made contracts depends on the financial condition of the company at the time of the managers' retirement, they are more reassuring than a promise. Also, they can be negotiated when the manager comes to work or after a trial period, when he has acquired some negotiating strength and not when he is old or ill with limited job mobility.

The danger of a deferred compensation or retirement plan is that it may keep executives around long after they have served their purpose. Further, the time between the performance (this year) and the enjoyment of the benefits (years later) is so great that it is unreasonable to expect anyone to act to improve profits now for a distant payoff. Hence, deferred compensation becomes the "golden handcuffs" that hold executives who have little more to contribute. The deficiency is not balanced by a strong advantage. Vested interests can no longer hold strong executives.

Employee stock ownership plans (ESOP's). A program that has attracted attention disproportionate to the number of actual installations is ESOP. The assumption behind ESOP is that stock in the company can be used to move people to higher performance. And in truth, stock ownership is attractive.

However, the strategy has its own problems. Who is to get how many shares, at what price, over what period of time are some of the problems, and they are complicated in the smaller company by the need to have buy-sell agreements.

In most cases it is better to give designated key people a chance to buy stock or to distribute stock rather than cash (or in addition to cash) as part of a bonus arrangement. Since the sale or distribution of stock has many technical requirements, managers should consult with their tax counsel before initiating a plan.

An ESOP can be attractive because it permits the use of pretax dollars to pay off loans which ordinarily require after-tax dollars, facilitates distributing corporate stock in proportion to the salary levels of employees, and may make redemption of the stock of retiring or deceased stockholders more financially digestible.

Because most employees prefer cash to the stock of a narrowly held company, the plan should provide for the payment of cash for the corporate shares that employees are entitled to receive when they leave the company. Like all aspects of an ESOP which must satisfy IRS requirements, this part of the transaction must be carefully planned. Common provisions are that if an employee (or his beneficiary) wants to sell corporate stock received from an ESOP, he must offer the company the right of first refusal to acquire it on the same basis as a competitive offer and that the corporation will be obligated to purchase at some formula-determined price any shares offered by an employee or his beneficiary within a prescribed period.

Eligibility for an ESOP cannot be limited to key people but must be set up on a nondiscriminatory basis to cover a wide spectrum of employees. ESOP eligibility rules are substantially the same as those of other deferred compensation plans. Recent changes have expanded the voting rights of plan participants.

The evidence is not yet in on the motivational effects of ESOP's, but it seems reasonable that the deferment of benefits to retirement or termination of employment and the inability to target stock ownership limit the value of ESOP's as a fringe benefit.

As a means of disposing of stock and making partial sales of stock without incurring severe tax problems, an ESOP can help, subject to substantial limitations.

Participation in equity growth. There are many techniques for attracting and retaining managers through ownership. Briefly summarized, stock ownership serves the psychological needs of some people; it can create a market for the stock of older shareholders at their retirement or death, and it can be the most equitable way of giving credit for contribution to profit.

Shadow stock (stock appreciation rights). Although participation in the equity growth of one's employer is a common desire, stock options (qualified or nonqualified) and stock warrants are rarely used in smaller companies. Outright sale of stock in significant amounts requires cash or long-term obligations. In addition to the financial problems of employees' eventually having to pay for the stock, other problems, such as the shifting shoals of the tax treatment of options, have made smaller companies wary of stock options and warrants.

Shadow (phantom or performance) stock or stock appreciation rights have been developed to serve the healthy wish to participate in equity growth. Although the mechanics and computations differ, the technique generally works this way: Selected, key employees are credited with a share of the firm's increase in value. Since no shares are actually issued, the plan avoids complications related to minority stockholder interests, voting rights, dividends, redemption, and so forth. Key employees given shadow or performance stock (or appreciation rights) usually receive a contract or verbal promise that they will benefit from the increase in the firm's worth.

This increase is expressed as a change in the book value from the time of granting to termination of employment. No corporate deductions are taken, no personal income is received until payments are made, at which point they are ordinary income, not capital, transactions. The employee invests no money and enjoys none of the privileges of being a stockholder; on the other hand, he does not have to pay for the stock. And he has a personal interest in improving the firm's long-range (as opposed to year-to-year) profits.

Example. Jack Harder is the thirty-six-year-old marketing vice-president of the Synaturf Company whose book value is $4 million. The company has been averaging 10 percent ROI. Harder's salary and annual cash bonus (based on corporate results and his achievement of personal objectives) total $45,000. The amount is adequate as compensation and for him to live on, but his growing family and rising standard of living have not allowed him to accumulate more than $10,000 in liquid savings.

Harder would like to own some Synaturf stock but the controlling family is reluctant to sell shares outside the family. Even if the family were willing to sell shares to Harder, the number he could buy, without a recapitalization, is so small as to be insignificant.

Because the family wants to retain Harder's interest in the company's long-term success, they offered, and Harder accepted, a stock appreciation contract which promised to pay him 3 percent of the increase in the company's book value—from $4 million to the amount at the year-end prior to the termination of his employment. His rights to the appreciation vested over ten years, at 10 percent a year, and were payable over the same number of years as he had earned in vesting. If the company should be worth $10 million in ten years (and Harder left), his 3 percent share of the $6 million increase would be $180,000, payable over ten years. The company's owners also left open the possibility that they might increase the number of Harder's stock appreciation rights.

Harder now had the same interest in increasing the company's value as the shareholders. When received, his payments will be ordinary income. They also depend on his staying with the company. But he is free of any obligation to invest in the firm beyond his time and effort and can diversify his financial interests.

Other provisions of typical shadow stock or appreciation right agreements may include:

□ Limits on owner-manager salaries in determing value, to avoid the obvious exposure of a nonstockholder to the reduction in net income from controlling stockholders' excessive compensation.
□ A formula for determining annual stock value when book value is inappropriate.
□ A tie-in of the payments with a reasonable convenant not to compete.
□ Granting phantom common shares, rather than a percentage of increased net worth, whose number can be adjusted with changing corporate needs and executive evaluation.
□ Crediting dividends paid on issued shares to the phantom shares.

PERSONAL ITEMS OR PERQUISITES ("PERKS")

These items are related primarily to personal circumstances or taste and provide smaller-company managers with the greatest opportunities to be imaginative and to express their management style. Examples are automobiles; combination business-personal trips; use of facilities, apartments, and planes; extra life insurance; membership in country, athletic, and eating clubs; flexible working hours; investment in off-balance-sheet related partnerships; and time for the fulfillment of a manager's personal interests—for example, in art, antiques, or community service.

As individualism is more and more expressed in the type of job or work that young, bright managers choose, smaller companies can increasingly use the fringe benefit packages to attract and keep a sought-after manager without upsetting regular administrative routines.

Officers' and directors' liability insurance. This type of insurance offers financial comfort at a modest cost. It does not protect against gross negligence or criminal activity, nor does it ensure that an officer or director will not be involved in a suit with possible taint to his reputation. But it provides some assurance that personal assets are safe from attack because of corporate affiliation.

Personal liability insurance. Personal liability insurance is normally a corporate deduction and a personal income item for the covered manager. We mention it because the corporate employer can often purchase personal umbrella liability coverage more easily and cheaply than the individual can. It is a service to the manager who wants it and may keep key people freer of outside hassles.

Company apartment, plane, private rail car, dining room. Use of such facilities tells much about management style. No moral judgment is implied; some businesses can appropriately use these facilities for customers, vendors, or prospects. When their use is more heavily weighted in the direction of the personal enjoyment of company officers, a management style of rewarding status emerges. Care in utilizing this kind of fringe is also necessary because of the IRS's sensitivity to nonbusiness use and the tightened rules concerning entertainment facilities. Our experience is that unless they are carefully monitored (which is in itself time-consuming), these benefits tend to become sources of internal friction and alienation within the organization (who is in or out of the inner circle becomes a major preoccupation). In one company that had a valid business use for three planes to move executives efficiently among 25 retail locations, the president's scheduling of the planes to make sure that he had one for weekend personal use took so much of his time that the planes became a corporate joke. The situation violates a canon: to matter, fringes cannot be objects of ridicule.

A corporate dining room may suffer the same problem of executive privilege and status setting. On the positive side (especially where there are limited local facilities for the type of gracious entertaining of customers that is appropriate to the relationship), a private dining room can be a relatively inexpensive way of complimenting customers for their wisdom in choosing your company as a source of supply. To benefit from the fringe, make sure availability is not decided on the basis of the pecking order, and that bookings are always honored. It won't hurt customer relations to have the president take a client or banker to the local beanerie because "my production manager has the dining room tied up today."

Club memberships. When applicable to business use and acceptable according to IRS rules, club memberships are motivating fringes to most executives. Unless the smaller firm's headquarters are in a city where it is almost obligatory for everyone in a social-economic level to belong to a club, we suggest that membership be one of the choice salad-bar benefits: Let those managers who want to join do so; the expense of membership should be a personal expense, deductible if proper by the executive. The company should reimburse the executive for valid business items, as it would for any entertainment expense. Those who do not want to join a club can choose another benefit.

Company cars. In leanly run smaller companies only those who can justify the use of a company car in accordance with IRS rules have them, and others are reimbursed for mileage or a combination of fixed monthly costs for having the car available and a small mileage charge for actual use.* When an executive car is used *primarily* for nondeductible commutation and personal activity, it sends out a clear message from management to employees. Since style more than substance is involved, before you decide how you want to handle the question of executive cars, consider the impression that your decision on the type of car and the level of business use is likely to have on all employees, not only those who will use the cars.

Where company-paid cars are appropriate, let individual taste select the car to be used. One executive may want an American-made compact, another a $30,000 foreign sports car. Since the company is paying dollars for car use, not for a specific vehicle, it should set dollar limits on car expense for each manager, or better, let each

---

*For example, $150 a month plus 8¢ a mile for variable costs.

manager include the cost of his car—whatever model and whatever use he makes of it—in *his* choice of fringe benefits.

Failure to identify dollars caused a misunderstanding among three doctors, whose agreement called for the partnership to buy each one a car. That wording was changed to dollar value after one doctor bought a Masserati, one a Cadillac, and the third a stripped Ford.

Financial Consulting. Many smaller-company managers are so busy with their jobs that they do not take the time to plan their estate and personal finance programs. Through their CPA, tax counsel, investment firm, or firms specializing in such planning, the company can make professional services available to key employees. Most tax practitioners agree that a strict interpretation of the rules requires that the value of these services be includable in the executive's income. Practice is less strict.

Corporate buying power. This fringe benefit enables employees to purchase personal items at a discount. If the company's normal purchasing requirements include items which managers might use personally, the company can act as purchasing agent to make a better buy. Personal cars, building supplies, and office equipment are items which the company can buy for a lower price and then resell to employees with minimum clerical effort.

Chauffeur. An obvious status symbol, a chauffeur can free a busy executive for productive, time-saving work. As in all deductions, the business purpose of the expense must be justified.

In a law firm where the senior partner had to drive two hours daily between his home and two offices, other partners insisted on hiring a chauffeur to free him to study, dictate, and phone. A cost-benefit analysis showed that at the standard billing rate at which the senior partner's time was charged to clients, time freed by the chauffeur produced $50,000 of additional billing.

Interest-free loans to nonstockholders. These can tide an executive over financial squeezes and provide him with extra money when he cannot otherwise obtain the cash he needs. Use with discretion and provide for reasonable but sure payback.

Lump sum salary increase or bonus. Many executives do not have a chance to handle a substantial amount of cash. Companies have experimented with letting a manager take as a lump sum an annual salary increase or a bonus which is traditionally spread over a year. The executive signs a written agreement to repay the unearned proportionate share if he leaves before the year is out. This program implies trust; it also implies that an executive knows best when and how he wants *his* money. The cost to implement the program is only the company's loss of the use of the funds.

Off-balance-sheet partnerships. Companies that have need for any type of plant or equipment, from buildings to computers, can rent the necessary asset from a partnership consisting of owner-managers, their families, or key executives. In brief, the operating company leases assets, at an arm's-length negotiation on rent, from a partnership consisting of any of the people mentioned above. The partnership invests a minimum amount of cash and finances the asset from the purchaser or a lending institution, pledging it and the operating lease as collateral. Rent flows to the partnership, the loans are paid, and the surplus cash and some tax benefits are distributed to the partners.

Check with your tax counsel for the IRS conditions relating to the investment and financing of rental partnerships.

Being invited into a rental partnership is a sign of acceptance; only those expected to stay with the company are asked. A popular way of saving income taxes, rental partnerships are especially useful when managers' children are included. They are an aboveboard way of paying tax-deductible dollars to people who are not on the payroll.

Contributions. At this writing, deductible corporate contributions equal to 5 percent of the pretax net income were allowed. Amounts available can be spread among key executives to satisfy their own charitable obligations, as long as the amounts paid are clearly designated as corporate deductions. Another use of contributions is to concentrate the bulk of the available amount in one charitable organization, especially one in which a member of the company has a public and important position. There is an intangible benefit in being able to direct corporate contributions so they have social clout.

Personal items and working conditions. If corporate efficiency (not past policy or bureaucratic consistency) permits, the smaller company can cater to managers' individual tastes. Office decor, antiques or art, flexible working hours, working at home, a nonconforming dress code, vacations taken in days or weeks and when the family wants—these are some examples of putting a personal stamp on work.

To the extent that managers of closely held firms can stretch the permissible ways in which people can perform to their tastes, the message comes through that individuals and results count, not routine.

Openness, participation, involvement. One of the most powerful fringe benefits is seldom so regarded: allowing each key person to feel that he had a share in making the strategic decisions. Being in on things, being asked to express an opinion, being told of problems as soon as they arise—these are all signs of trust and importance. Nothing gets closer to the respect management has for its key people than to ask them first what they feel is a proper salary, and for what reasons. This approach reverses the usual message of one-direction communication of salary changes and discretionary bonus. By asking the employee what he thinks he should be earning, top management does not abdicate either its responsibility for being fair nor its power to make the decision. It subtly changes the salary discussion from a monologue to a dialogue between almost equals.

Acknowledge the mystery of motivation—we do not know why people act as they do; nor, in most cases, do they. A nonfinancial reward such as being in on things costs nothing. Include it in your list of motivators.

Attendance at conventions and meetings. Trips to exotic places to attend conventions or meetings are properly used as rewards, and sometimes as incentives, for achieving a level in the organization or a sales or profit goal. The major drawback of offering such trips for those who hit the target is that the losers (usually the majority) may lose motivation. However, that can be controlled (if not eliminated) by making the chance of success open to everyone and by providing that one person's success is not at someone else's expense. Watch the limitations on the number of trips and deductible expenses for foreign conventions.

Resort locales for annual meetings. If you have an active, independent board of directors or advisory committee, consider holding at least one meeting a year in a resort or other pleasant location where business can be discussed but nonbusiness hours can be enjoyed. Since smaller companies generally do not overpay their outside advisers, the additional cost of the annual retreat will be modest, and the busy, competent people most eligible for a board or advisory committee may be more inclined to work with a smaller company which is imaginative in when and where it holds its meetings.

Sabbaticals. Just as the academic fraternity has developed the concept of the sabbatical to free a teacher for independent work or psychic battery-recharging, forward-looking companies are considering sabbaticals for their key managers. A sabbatical of 3 to 12 months can expand horizons, permit life-goal reassessments, and bring the executive back with strengthened commitment. If reassessment results in a decision not to return to the same job after 25 years, the sabbatical will have prepared the way for a new life, in itself a good thing.

Although our experience with sabbaticals in smaller companies is limited, we have found that offering a sabbatical is an attractive, competitively unique inducement to young managers for whom work is not the only purpose in life.

Disallowed expenses. A corporate agreement on disallowed expenses, especially for substantial shareholders, may be self-serving but should be part of every company's minutes. An employee who is a minority or nonowning shareholder is usually better off not having to return amounts disallowed—the tax rate is under 100 percent. See the example in "Reasonable Compensation," Chapter 6.

Cafeteria plans. The 1978 Revenue Act made substantial changes in cafeteria plans, those permitting the employee to choose his own fringe benefits. Because experience with the rules is limited, be guided by your tax counsel's current interpretation.

A cafeteria plan is a written agreement permitting employees to choose among two or more benefits (taxable and nontaxable), but not including deferred compensation. The usual, now familiar eligibility standards (taken from ERISA rules) apply.

Among the positive changes the act brought to cafeteria plans is the clarification that a participant will not be taxed just because he has choices among the benefits offered. As usual, highly compensated individuals are excluded from this exemption if the plan is discriminatory. ("Highly compensated" means both those who are eligible because of their pay level or status and those who receive special benefits.)

You may have some latitude in the scale of benefits since a plan will not be discriminatory if the total benefits, as a *percentage* of contribution, are about the same for all participants. Specific benefits mentioned as nontaxable in a cafeteria plan are group term life insurance up to $50,000, disability benefits, accident and health insurance coverage, and group legal service.

Small-company executives wanting to expand benefits available to top managers may still do so by attaching an after-tax dollar cost to each choice and letting the manager choose what he wants. If the benefits made available included such items as the type of automobile, additional taxable insurance premiums, club membership, or time off, the company would still be able to individualize part of its fringe package.

For items required to be made available to all eligible employees, highly paid (and ostensibly valuable) employees could be favored by relating benefits to the compensation level.

TIMING AND ADMINISTRATIVE CONSIDERATIONS

The manager has limited control over the basic fringe benefits. Most coverages are now universally expected; it is rare to find a company that does not have ordinary medical-surgical and life insurance coverages. A fair percentage of firms have major medical insurance. Because of the competitive disadvantage a company would face if it tried to attract or retain good people without these benefits, it has little choice but to include them. If it is to compete for the best human resources, it must have the expanded coverages.

Far greater discretion can be exercised in respect to the next level of fringes:

☐ Offering life insurance that provides the possibility of continuing a lifestyle to which the family of a deceased employee has become accustomed.

☐ A retirement program (usually with the longest vesting ERISA allows) to supplement Social Security payments.

☐ Disability insurance beyond legal minimums and inclusive of accidents or illnesses independent of the work situation.

☐ A car that offers personal advantages in addition to those essential to corporate use.

☐ Membership in business-related clubs or associations; and so forth.

These fringes are often targeted to individuals rather than made generally available, and they therefore must be treated with as much wisdom as discretion. They invite invidious comparison. Clear rules of why people are included must be laid down, cold-blooded analysis of the rules' effects on management style and tone must be made, and where the effects are negative, adjustments must be made before the rules are made public—as in the end they have to be.

Once adopted, both fringe benefit groups are extremely difficult to drop. They become expected, depended on, and they cause disproportionate resentment when reduced. The lesson is clear: Add the second tier of benefits with great care, being as sure as you can that you can continue to afford them under most economic conditions. Even if you juggle the benefits in Solomon-like wisdom, adding value to some while subtracting it from others, you will face morale problems if you change them.

Examples. One small-company president decided to avoid the problem of choosing and changing benefits. His incentive bonus program was the source of all voluntary benefits, including the most basic medical insurance coverage. The decision as to the choice of the benefits was entirely in the hands of an employee-elected committee. The larger the incentive bonus, the greater the benefits. The owner's answer to the request for broader benefits was simple: If you want more benefits, earn more; it's all up to you.

In a second case, a committee of employees was elected to distribute the benefits, the cost limit of which was set by management.

Both techniques used the democratic process to reduce the differences of opinion common to the handling of benefits and, incidentally, to remove the paternalism usually associated with (and resented by the more resourceful employees) top-management-administered benefit programs.

Administration of fringes is at two levels. We have discussed the first: decisions on the scope and type of fringes. This is usually done by top management or by a group of employees. The second aspect is the daily administration. Largely clerical, the administration of the benefit program is one of the regular sensitive contacts between management and employees which can be a dissatisfier. Done well, benefit administration is invisible; done insensitively, it is an unnecessary cause of dissension. Pick a person to handle the paperwork who knows the program and can answer questions and handle routine efficiently, fairly, and with taste.

In a company with fewer than 300 people it is rare to find a full-time personnel officer. The personnel functions are handled part-time by one person or divided among several, and benefits under such arrangements are seldom well handled. In one company three people conducted interviews of applicants; two others did reference-checking (one for the office and one for the plant); and the direct supervisor, as usual, had his say on final selection. The result of the split in responsibility is inconsistency and lack of professionalism in firms otherwise well managed.

Because no one manager had the requisite skills or sensitivity to handle the whole job in a client firm that was justifiably proud of the quality of their products, we recommended that a part-time personnel director be hired to handle all normal hiring, wage administration, and the special compensation functions. A half-day a week or a few days a month can extract enough extra value out of the activities to add to the profits of a smaller company.

Personnel consultants are available on a regular, part-time basis. Other sources are moonlighters from larger companies or local professors with consulting experience. The value of the professional regular part-timer is that he gets to know the organization, his candidate contact and selection skills are higher and consistent, and he brings a fresh approach to the whole personnel function.

A part-time personnel expert can bring into the company new ideas from many sources on incentives, executive salary levels, and the comparative cost of different fringe benefits. The cost of paying for such professionalism in most cases will be paid back many times by better hirings (more competence for the money or less money for the competences needed), fewer dissatisfactions over benefits, and in most cases, a marked reduction in unnecessary turnover.

One other valuable contribution should be mentioned: The biggest personnel decision is the first—selection. It is rare to find a nonexpert who is good at it; it takes special skill to define the job and the qualifications needed, organize an interview, ask probing questions, watch for signs of stress and truth distortion, identify strengths, check references thoroughly, and then balance the information to evaluate the relative prospects of several candidates.

Since most small companies hire key people infrequently, they can benefit from the continuing relationship of a professional who knows the internal atmosphere and norms of behavior and the idiosyncrasies of key managers. Selection errors will be fewer; salary and career expectations of new people can be discussed. In sum, to a desirable applicant the company shows that it wants to be professional.

8

Summary

IN this chapter we summarize the ideas we have put forth about compensating key executives in smaller companies and offer our forecast of trends and influences most likely to affect compensation in the future. Such forecasts are chancy at best, but anyone interested or involved in compensation planning should make forecasts for two reasons: (1) compensation plans are essentially flexible plans laid for the intermediate term, two to five years, and therefore should be made readily responsive to future changes in the firm's environment and should not establish precedents that are hard to change; and (2) compensation plans, like all other plans, should be designed to set the firm apart from its competitors—to help establish, extend, and maintain the firm's uniqueness.

REVIEW OF BASICS

Compensation in the closely held or smaller company is a crucial if limited tool, as all management tools are. Therefore, to make the most effective use of compensation, it must be fitted to the company's economic function, long-range goals, and total strategic picture. If those are not well established, tested, and clear, compensation will not make a great deal of difference in the firm that plans it. Where compensation is not highly integrated with the other forces at work in a firm, you will do just as well to pay on an ad hoc, copycat basis.

Getting answers to searching questions is integral to good compensation planning. Following are a few such questions that may set directions for raising the profit contributions of compensation planning.

1. What do you have to do especially well to succeed in your business? What are your strengths? How well do they measure against those of your competitors?

2. How are you different from your actual and potential competitors? A small company consciously has to identify, preserve, and possibly extend its uniqueness. The value of the uniqueness is market-based and is evidenced in the occupation and exploitation of market niches in which the firm offers superior products and/or services, which in turn create the working atmosphere that is tough, demanding, and rewarding for those who want to work. The effective compensation plan is the most visible and durable driving force behind the establishment, preservation, and extension of a firm's uniqueness.

3. Having identified your competitive position, the products, services, or custoner areas in which you can be superior, and the working atmosphere that affects individual and group contribution, you can now ask the staffing and organizational questions: Do you have the organizational structure that best serves your markets, fosters your strengths, counters your weaknesses, helps make and keep you unique? Is your organization arranged in the light of any identification of the sensitive locations for superior decision making?

4. Are your key people receiving information in accordance with their needs (and to keep them from spending time to get it)? Does that information also serve the performance-auditing and control needs of the company? To make competitively superior decisions, the right people need the right information at the right time. They also have to be directed and their performance monitored in the right way (key people can be negatively as well as positively *key*). They need challenge and satisfaction, but within balanced controls.

5. Are you paying your key people in accordance with their abilities to contribute to the firm's strengths and uniqueness, for capacities to seek out the firm's problems and opportunities and to

improve upon the firm's performance? In short, are you paying for that form of individualism we call originality (thinking of things before others think of them), entrepreneurship (initiating action before others do), leadership (getting people to act before others do)?

Obtaining answers to such questions is essential to devising compensation plans which add to the forward momentum and profitability of the firm. The answers are also part of the information base needed to integrate strategies, organization, and compensation planning—the integration itself is a qualification of the value of compensation planning.

In doing the actual planning, remember to use compensation to attract and retain the right people, to make staying unattractive for those who do not fit, and to permit sideways or downward moves within the organization to retain worthwhile people who have either been misplaced, lost their steam, or want to reduce or limit the scale of their efforts.

If you particularly need risk taking, growth, ambiguity handling, or fast response to change, look for tigers. To attract and direct tigers, design a compensation that rewards risk taking and punishes cautiousness (not forgetting the performance factor, of course). If you anticipate little or cannot handle much growth, expect little change, need tight cost control, then design a compensation system which rewards conservative and conserving administration. And don't get your people types mixed up—tigers don't make good maintenance executives, nor do detail- and control-oriented executives make good tigers.

In your compensation design work, be creative. Use the most imaginative list of rewards you can in support of the firm's objectives. Doing so, of course, implies that both goals and rewards are clear (ambiguity is a serious, often fatal, compensation disease). But keep some humility, too: although our knowledge of motivation and the relationship between performance and pay is growing, we have a lot to learn. We have sufficient evidence that compensation may affect performance if the reward is important to the person. And we know that, in most cases, pay *is* important.

The next step is to agree jointly in advance on the few key results by which a manager's performance will be measured. Easily said, this is the heart of the performance-pay problem: What results count in moving the organization ahead? Over what specific results does the individual manager have control? Are the measurements fair, achievable, clear, and the rewards worthwhile to *him*? Can his additional or different effort significantly affect the quality of those results? To the manager, are the rewards worth the additional effort, the changed social relationships, or the personal sacrifices?

Always keep in mind when planning or tinkering with compensation that, in the same way that a budgeting, cost control, internal communications, or MBO program cannot stand alone, neither can a compensation plan. Compensation should support and be a part of the fabric of a management philosophy. The other threads include the key management group's ethical values, their vision of the company, feelings about disclosure and openness, sense of equity as to who produces and shares in profits, customer orientation, and their willingness to acknowledge differences in performance and pay.

FUTURE TRENDS

What future trends are likely to have an impact on compensation it is hard to estimate, but the following discussion touches on those areas that could affect compensation.

Wage controls are a tempting political move. In a period of disturbing inflation, they give the illusion of stability without necessarily being effective. If inflation prompts wage controls, it will be important that small companies muster political pressure to reduce stifling paperwork procedures by seeking exemption from the reporting process or from the controls themselves. In anticipation of wage controls, to the extent corporate cash requirements and compensation reasonableness permit, executive compensation policy should lean toward the upper range of salaries and bonuses.

Managers at all levels will become even more sensitive to inflation and will expect routine inflation-equalizing raises. Any increase in the quality and level of a dialogue on pay and performance should be healthy. In addition to the involvement, the more openness and joint planning in the setting of goals and rewards, the greater the effectiveness of the compensation program.

Small companies with only a few organizational and pay levels may face the loss of good people who are prevented from moving up to higher earnings and who therefore may move to larger organizations with more pay levels and a greater chance to earn more.

The 1978 Tax Reform Act attack on fringe benefit misuse (which had as many ethical as tax revenue aspects) may have been only one in a series of such moves. With the bulk of the tax-paying and voting public unable to enjoy the visible fringes available to corporate officers, it is easy (and therefore likely) for politicians to wave the flag of fringe benefit "reform" as a rallying point for tax reform (and reelection). Expect continued attacks and prepare to use current and deferred cash payments to supplement possible reduction in fringes.

The application of behavioral knowledge about the place of work in people's lives will expand. We see two trends:

1. Work will be downgraded to a necessary but minor part of an individual's total life. People will work primarily for economic reasons; loyalty to their work and their employers will be limited; management's attempts to involve workers will be looked at skeptically as manipulative. Life satisfactions will be sought outside the work area. This scenario will be most common at the office and factory level and for routine work of middle managers.

2. Higher-level managers will continue to find personal challenge and satisfaction and a major part of their self-image from their work.

If the inherent satisfactions from work decline, compensation may become a larger factor in retaining people and directing behavior. If work satisfactions are largely from those things that can be bought by the price of work (goods, freedom, leisure), then compensation increases relatively in influencing managerial and other worker behavior.

Before abandoning the massive findings on human needs and the job, managers should find out what their people want. Feedback from questionnaires and regular individual listening sessions may help identify what parts of a job and the work environment can be changed and where pay fits. Currently, pay is not the major problem with most employees.* If the unhappiness relating to achievement, fairness, and recognition is not or cannot be dealt with satisfactorily, pay is both a logical target for dissatisfaction and a management tool to allay the discontent.

Computers will increase centralized decision making and reduce the number of managers who deserve compensation recognition. Pay

*M. R. Cooper, B. S. Morgan, P. M. Foley, and L. B. Kaplan, "Changing Employee Values," *Harvard Business Review*, Jan.–Feb. 1979.

and other individualized rewards will continue to be used to direct behavior. Managers will have to deal with a broad declining satisfaction from work, the result in part of the gap between what people expect and what they get out of their work. Work frustration may result in new and tougher worker organization, including middle managers. The alternative has been mentioned: People will direct their interest and energies outside their jobs. Both conditions will complicate management and muddy up the waters of the pay-performance problem.

The second possible change, deriving from behavioral research both in large company and laboratory experiments, may be an increase in the influences of groups in the conduct of business affairs. We anticipate, therefore, the need for increasing concern in compensation planning with group incentives and rewards. If we are correct, more care will be needed in choosing group members as groups will have greater autonomy in making decisions on their work standards, personnel codes, and reward system: how the group performance is to be measured, and how the rewards are to be distributed. Small-company managers who early familiarize themselves with group dynamics and who invest the time to find out what they are and how to apply them may well generate competitive advantages for their firms.

The advantages of employing groups lie in the logical division of products and services into small enough groups whose output can be seen as a whole and for which the group can be accountable and compensated.

Aside from getting a better understanding of your own firm and its competitive environment through the questions listed above, don't forget the larger world in which your firm lives. We make compensation planning assumptions that the U.S. economy is unlikely to grow in real terms at more than 3 percent annually, but that the internal drive for growth, to satisfy ego and organizational needs, will not shrink proportionately.

If our assumptions are correct, companies will face increasing competition as they cannibalize existing markets and fight over key accounts. We also would assume, with lower probability, to be sure, that national trade barriers will decline to reflect geopolitical polarization, with the result that small firms will then face increasing international competition (already begun in this country) and will have to seek out opportunities to expand overseas. European and

Asian firms have historically looked beyond their boundaries for markets. In their own interest, U.S. firms will now have to do the same, and in the last two decades have succeeded in intensifying their penetration in overseas markets. Success in such efforts will depend in part on adopting skills in utilizing compensation techniques yielding rewards to which they are now unaccustomed.

9

Case Studies

THE 12 case studies in this chapter (all of which occurred in actual companies whose names were altered to preserve their anonymity) demonstrate how theory and practice are combined. They deal with many of the compensation issues faced in smaller companies. Note the following points:

1. The political and emotional content of compensation is always close to the surface. Thus, no matter how "correct" a particular solution may seem to be, it may have to be adjusted in consideration for the status and influence of certain key people.

2. Family relations have to be treated carefully, and satisfying them may contradict some of the rules of paying for performance.

3. Stock ownership is a powerful influence in setting pay.

4. The company should come first.

5. Every company is unique and changing.

CASE STUDY: APS COMPANY

APS sells $6 million of supplies to the construction industry through a dozen direct salespersons. As a distributor it also rents heavy equipment. The president and sole stockholder had invited a group of strong, competent outsiders to become his board of directors and guide him. He used this group to introduce budgets and the ROI concept, assist in making major expansion decisions, and advise him on how his job should change as the company grew.

The compensation program had not been changed for years. Salaries and the fringe benefit program were competitive, but all raises and bonuses were discretionary. No employee was able to state what he had to do to earn more or why he had received one amount rather than another for his last raise or bonus.

Following are excerpts from our report. The summary "rules" at the beginning of the report are applicable to almost any company. Violating them risks implementation of any plan.

The "standard rules" for any incentive compensation program are:

1. The company comes first. Growth plans require cash and the company should be protected through sufficient retained earnings to withstand errors, mistakes, and uncertainties, before any bonus pay is distributed.

2. A win/lose situation is destructive. The incentive system should not permit anyone to earn more because someone earns less.

3. Where performance is identifiable and controllable, managers who produce extra results should be rewarded significantly. Where performance is hard to separate and the corporate results are primarily a team effort, then a group incentive is best. Whatever system is used, it is necessary to evaluate performance and not leave distribution entirely to an impersonal formula.

4. Discretionary bonuses are usually demotivating. They remove control of performance and the rewards for doing it from the hands of the individual to the mysterious realm of the grantor, or boss. With this limitation, it is still necessary to set some part of the incentive aside for discretion, to reward the person whose special effort could not be anticipated. The rarely used benefit of discretionary bonuses, therefore, is to reward the "how" of a job as well as the "what."

5. An MBO program for some of the key managers should not conflict with the compensation program. Compensation must be an integral part of management practices.

Since basic pay levels are reasonable, individuals can move within the ranges of their jobs as they achieve the MBO standards. Corporate profitability is the soundest method of rewarding the group's extra efforts.

A formula was proposed in which a pretax return of 30 percent of the net worth at the beginning of the year was excluded from the bonus computation, and an increasing portion of the excess was contributed to a bonus pool. The distribution of the bonus was not helped by a ranking of people in terms of their contribution to profits. The ranking revealed no pattern; it was parochial and largely influenced by the work and place of the rater.

Although the ranking procedure, with its perception of those working together, almost always adds to the evaluation, in some companies people do not know what others do. Their rankings are invalid. In a professional organization (law, architecture, engineering, accounting, management consultants) the organization of work is usually a series of parallel lines in which people do the same thing for different clients but rarely have professional contact with each other. Evaluations are rarely more than reactions to superficial personality traits, past relationships, or gossip.

The president set his salary and bonus at any reasonable (to the IRS) level. For several reasons he participated in the corporate bonus:

☐ He is unanimously considered to be the most important factor in producing corporate profit.
☐ His participation reduces the possible argument that the group bonus is excessive.
☐ It shows the other participants that the president shares only in profits when earned, and thus reinforces the team effort concept. The top ten employees were awarded specific bonus percentages; 15 percent was set aside for discretion.

The discretionary 15 percent is important. The predetermined percentages should be based on each person's contribution to profit: his job, leverage in affecting results, and effectiveness in doing the job. The best of ten warehousemen or clerks in the company is unlikely to have the same effect on profits as an average purchasing agent, marketing manager, or controller.

The discretionary 15 percent is provided for the special performance, problem, effort, unpleasantness that you cannot anticipate. Its appropriateness should be obvious to everyone. It can be given to one or more people or, if no one is an obvious candidate, it can be left in the general bonus pool or retained as corporate earnings.

The company's sales and profit goals should be tied to individual performance goals. Although making a profit is healthy and acceptable, for many people it is not enough. They want to know how the company will be run, its place in the market, and where they fit. Some of these issues are not clear to managers because they may not be clear to the owners.

When the key issues have been written and discussed with top managers, work out where each person fits. This exercise must be done *before* starting an MBO program to avoid possible conflicts between individual priorities and corporate aims.

Compensation makes most sense when it rewards the key, unique, competitively advantageous reasons for a company's success.

CASE STUDY: BC COMPANY

The BC company is a manufacturer with annual sales of approximately $40 million, 700 employees, growth and profit rates considerably above the industry's. The president owns less than 3 percent of the stock and has no options. He has been responsible for developing a management team which is not dependent on any one person.

Because his older brother is chairman of the board and the major stockholder with more than 40 percent of the shares, both brothers and several members of the board of directors felt that it would be helpful to get an outsider's opinion of an appropriate salary and bonus for the president. Continued extraordinary sales growth and high return on investment rates were crucial to the company's long-range goals. As is so often the case in well-run companies, top managers considered compensation as a function of corporate strategy, not a separate procedure. The consultant's suggestions were divided into several key areas, as shown here:

Assumption and Facts

1. The base salary should fall within a range paid to CEO's of companies of comparable size and industries. (Comment: To compensate for an adequate performance as an asset maintainer.)
2. Any bonus should be based on profitability and sales rate

growth greater than industry averages. (Comment: Key factors in the company's five-year growth plan.)

3. Because the company is an issuer of its own stock, traded over the counter, counsel advised that the stock cannot be used to compensate the president without registration. Stock could be made available for compensation purposes as part of future registrations.

4. If the registration requirements are met, the executive can choose the proportions of stock or cash he wants to receive.

5. The company's net income, sales growth, and self-financing goals are higher than commonly available national and industry history and projections. Achievement of the goals would represent extraordinary performance and be worthy of extraordinary reward.

6. Adjustment to the president's base and incentive pay is proper as a matter of equity more than as a factor in causing him to act differently.

External Standards

Selected external standards were taken from several sources. The data in Table 3 are from recent proxy statements of nonregulated firms with sales in the company's approximate range or larger. None approached BC's ROI or growth rate.

Table 3. Data from proxy statements of nonregulated firms (in thousands).

Company	Annual Sales	Net Income	CEO Remuneration
1	$26,000	$ 550	$112
2	55,000	3,100	115
3	42,000	1,700	200
4	65,000	3,700	120
5	23,000	(1,000)	100
6	20,000	700	100
7	50,000	3,100	115

The most recent Financial Executive Institute Biennial Survey of Executive Compensation listed $115,000 as the average total compensation of the CEO of companies in BC's industry classification (with $25–$100 million sales volume). Of the total executives covered, 80 percent received a bonus (included in the $115,000); the average bonus was 53 percent of base salary.

For all companies in the survey, the FEI reported average total CEO compensation for $25–$50 million sales volume companies as $106,000.

Several critical points must be made to bring these figures into focus:

1. The amounts were for 1976. Adjusted for inflation, current levels (1978) would be at least 25 percent higher. The FEI study reported an average 15 percent increase in total 1976 compensation. Combining 1977 and prospective 1978, the 1976 CEO figures would be adjusted to $125,000–$135,000. (Comment: Since surveys are always historical they are instantly partially obsolete. Adjust survey figures for inflationary changes.)

2. Consider the normal limitations of comparisons between reported figures and those of any individual firm:

☐ The report is not based on standard random sampling techniques and therefore may be statistically biased.
☐ The job of *an* executive, his responsibility, and profit contribution are not explained by his title.

3. Finally, the survey does not differentiate profitability, market share, quality of earnings, sales growth, or other significant factors. Although these items will ultimately be revealed in the ROI, they are not even touched upon in most surveys. Performance and pay are therefore not related in survey results.

Another source of reasonableness is the Compensation Report of the Research Institute of America. For manufacturing companies with sales of $30–$45 million, the 1975 median CEO compensation was $75,000, upper quartile $101,000, and highest reported $229,000. Adjusted for inflation the 1978 median becomes $112,000 and the upper quartile $145,000. Again, profitability and sales growth data are excluded.

Recommendation

Based on these reported levels and BC's past and projected ROI and growth, a 1978 base salary of $135,000 was proposed for the president, with incentive bonus to be computed as follows:

The president's incentive bonus started when 80 percent of

budgeted sales and pretax income were achieved. To keep the plan simple, the bonus should be contingent on achieving both sales and income goals. Other key corporate financial goals—self-financed growth and a dividend payout equal to 35 percent of net income— are less subject to the chief executive's input than to decisions by the board of directors. They are therefore excluded from the bonus base.

For every percentage point the company earns over 80 percent of the planned sales and pretax profit, the president will be given a bonus of 2 percent of his salary. Although no limit is placed on the company's earnings or the market price of its stock, a limit of 75 percent of base pay was put on the president's bonus.

The choice of 80 percent of budgeted sales and pretax income as the starting point for incentive pay was based on BC's high targets of 20 percent annual sales growth and 16–20 percent pretax income on *sales*. These goals were far above normal growth and income rates. Even the 80 percent level (16 percent sales and 11–16 percent pretax income on sales) was higher than most companies budget or achieve.

If the president manages the company so that it earns its projected amounts, the company will be in the upper ranks of growth and profitability, and he will have deserved a bonus equal to 40 percent of his base pay.

Because corporate plans are set by the management group and approved by an independent board of directors, it is unlikely that the president could set low goals solely for selfish, bonus purposes.

CASE STUDY: DFR COMPANY

DFR distributes technical equipment and offers its customers repair and custom modification services. Annual sales are $2.5 million. The president, Dan Rogers, has applied many modern management techniques to raise the level of the company's performance. He is working on a management objectives program to be integrated with a revised compensation program.

Interviews with key people were aimed at discovering measurable and significant profit contribution factors: What does each manager do, or what standard of performance could he and the CEO agree on in the beginning of a period against which he could be measured and then compensated? There were few factors or results that were both significant and specifically identifiable or traceable to one individual rather than to overall corporate activity or team effort.

The ideal goal of any compensation program is to relate an individual's performance and his compensation. Although commissions based on sales or gross profit would seem to be a clear example of rewarding specific performance, they do not reflect the whole story of who creates the customer and the sale. Compare the insurance salesperson representing the Prudential Insurance Company and one representing a company started last year with the minimum legal investment. Certainly a prospect's acceptance of the Prudential salesperson is likely to be stronger.

Identifying the source of new business and the attribution of credit for annual results is not easy. Just as the human body does not function through the specialties of medicine, organizations do not function through the artificial breakdowns created by administrative titles. The breakdowns help develop understanding and specialization, but results are more often traced to group, historical, or inherited causes.

Let us review the problems in setting significant (not cosmetic or superficial) standards to motivate managers to be more productive. The following responses indicate the absence of individual performance measures on which to base an incentive program. (Comment: Although the following job titles are unique to the DFR Company, they are characteristic of the problems in developing performance measures.)

Controller. The only significant profit factor over which he has control is the level of accounts receivable outstanding, a basic part of his job that should be covered by salary. The decisions as to how much credit to give and the place of credit in selling are top-level management decisions.

The absurd result of a misdirected credit and collection policy could be no bad debts or no accounts receivable. Credit and collection are not isolated; they serve to sell goods and should not be measured only by the negatives of low days of sale in outstanding accounts receivable or no bad debts.

Profit may not be directly related to lower receivables or bad debts. If he carried it to an extreme as a measure of his performance, the controller would be motivated to give no credit or give it only to customers who paid in ten days. Both courses would be catastrophic.

Sales manager. His direct sales activities could be measured against the normal salesman's standards of gross margin dollars. However, he has more important tasks: to develop new salesmen, teach them to handle more sophisticated sales, and introduce the company into new areas. None of these tasks is subject to precise measurement, and all have a longer-than-one-year payoff. Agree on the key results expected:

☐ Reduce the number of direct sales contacts.
☐ Increase the number of accounts handled by the salesmen.
☐ Expand salesmen's knowledge.
☐ Open up new markets. Then base the sales manager's salary on the performance in these areas, using quantitative measures where possible.

Warehouse and shipping manager. He suggested the completion of special projects, control of warehouse costs, and maintenance of budget. Because the completion of special projects is part of his job, it is not normally compensated for specially. Warehouse costs are largely fixed labor. Warehouse activity is not a result of the manager's initiative but a reflection of sales level.

Measuring picked and packed lines per warehouseman, level of inventory, and number of outages might be compared with a standard, but since the data are not available, the cost of keeping track of actual against standard will be greater than the value of the output.

Telephone salesman. Ninety-nine percent of the calls telephone service people handle are initiated by customers who know what they want. A telephone solicitation program is too new to evaluate. It may be measurable and therefore includable in future individual incentives. (Comment: Expect compensation programs to change as the business changes and you develop more data on individual contributions.)

Special market salesman. He can be paid for his additional profit contribution from selling in new areas. If the company received commissions of 5–15 percent on his sales, pay him 5 percent of the commissions earned after the company has earned two and a half times his annual salary. This amount should recover the company's out-of-pocket costs and a fair return on its investment. If his sales come from general corporate effort or from contacts made by others, this arrangement would be unfair.

If he is responsible for his sales, the compensation program would motivate the special market salesman and cost the company nothing: The incentive bonus would be paid only from earnings it would not have had without the salesman's extra effort.

Service manager. His sales volume depends on installations sold by others and his and the salesmen's ability to convince owners to use DFR's service. The place of service in the overall strategy of selling equipment must be clear. Its profitability will differ based on whether it is a selling tool for major equipment sales or whether it is expected to stand on its own. (First, the business strategy; then the compensation program to support it.)

Group incentive. If team effort is the source of increased profits, then the best program is a group incentive based on corporate profits after providing for corporate needs and a return to the stockholder. The rate of sales growth is limited by the rate of return on invested capital, asssuming that the sales-to-assets and debt-to-net-worth ratios remain the same, the latter because of borrowing limits and liquidity comfort level. If you intend to increase sales by 25 percent, the company will need net income after taxes of at least 25 percent before it can safely distribute incentive compensation. After adding back interest cost the required pretax return on invested capital (ROIC) to support projected sales is 35 percent. (The company's needs, which include growth, come first.)

With that financial background, consider a specific formula:

1. Take the company's net worth and its long-term interest-bearing debt, $250,000, as the ROIC base. To sustain expected sales growth without adding disproportionately to debt, the company should earn 35 percent of that figure, or $87,500, before any bonus payment.

2. Earnings above $87,500 are assumed to have been earned by the top management group and then other personnel. Here is a proposed formula of the bonus on earnings over the base:

On the first $25,000: 10%
On the next $25,000: 15%
On the next $50,000: 20%
Over $100,000: 25%

3. The division of bonus earnings is more difficult than the

computation of the total amount because it requires personal evaluation. The CEO's bonus should be predetermined so that he cannot play games which would affect the profit.

Each manager was asked to rank the top people in the company in order of his contribution to profit. This ranking was amended by the objective evaluation of an outside consultant to produce the following bonus distribution:

President	20%
Managers	
Sales	12
Division	10
Warehouse and shipping	8
Telephone sales	7
Controller	5
Service	3
Other	20
Discretionary	<u>15</u>
Total	100%

4. The "other" category and the discretionary portion require explanation. Since the top seven people are not the sole contributors to corporate results, the bonus should include everyone (total of 25 employees). If management has properly evaluated all personnel and has no incompetents, then everyone adds to the operation. Below the manager level, the ranking procedure rarely works. A simpler technique is to pay the bonus share attributable to the nonmanager group in proportion to base salary.

Finally, profits record only financial results, not the problems overcome, the effort and training given, the imagination, or other nonfinancial help an individual contributed. Thus, the discretionary bonus.

The five top managers should identify candidates for the 15 percent discretionary bonus. If the appropriateness of the decision is questionable or if no one stands out, the amount should be added back to the bonus pool. Maximum bonus payments should be 50 percent of base salary.

5. Do not change the salesmen's compensation now. If selling effort is redirected by new marketing facts, salesmen's efforts will be more centrally directed. This change will affect compensation.

If the salesmen are largely independent, a commission arrangement makes sense because they are responsible for finding and
selling prospects to serve their and the company's needs. If the
company can control (or should control) the salesmen's activities,
through area and market assignments, or high-level and continuous
training and supervision, and if the company can direct the priorities
of the salesmen's day and reduce their freedom, a salary and bonus
arrangement is preferable. (First the strategy; then the compensation
program to back it.)

CASE STUDY: THE OTTER COMPANY

The Otter Company, a manufacturer of specialty chemical
products for the construction industry, is owned by five brothers.
Table 4 shows their positions and stock holdings in the company, as
well as their salaries and ages. The company has been in existence
for 40 years, with many ups and downs. Its recent financial history is
as follows (in thousands):

	Sales	Net Income
1979 (Most recent year)	$6,400	280
1978	5,000	200
1977	4,000	200

Table 4. Stock holdings, positions, salaries, and ages of company owners.

Brother	Percentage of Stock Held	Position	Salary	Age
A	35%	President	$60,000	55
B	18	Director of research	45,000	58
C	18	Foreign operations	57,000	53
D	18	Product manager	48,000	47
E	11	Credit-collections	30,000	62
	100%			

The current fiscal year is anticipated to show $8 million sales and
$750,000 in income before taxes and bonuses. In addition to the five
brothers, the active board of directors includes two strong indepen-

dent outsiders. Marketing, manufacturing, controllership, and a product are managed by four competent, nonfamily executives who have individual incentive plans.

Otter markets three different product lines, all based on secret proprietary (not patented) formulations. Most of the profits for the last few years were produced by one product which was developed over ten years by the director of research and the marketing manager, with the president's support. In the late 1960s and early 1970s the company was kept alive by profits earned in Europe, a market which has been flat and barely profitable for the last three years.

The company has a generous pension plan which will provide retirement benefits to the brothers from 50 percent to 100 percent of their current pay if they work to age 65.

Problems: the president felt that the system was unfair and unpleasant. He had to decide salary changes for his brothers and was caught in the middle of emotional relationships and vague or no performance standards. Further, although the brothers got along, they differed on the goals of compensation. Opinions included: Pay salaries according to family needs; when earned, distribute profits as bonuses proportionate to stock ownership; put the company's needs first; put the stockholders' desires first.

This case includes many typical family compensation and management issues. The fundamental question had never been resolved: Why was Otter in business? Was it to be managed as an entity separate from its family ownership, or was it primarily to serve the brothers' personal needs? If the former, compensation should be related to company need and performance. If family priorities come first, then personal style and need or stock ownerships (largely inherited from the father) would determine who received what.

A consultant's report suggested a compromise possibility: Give major consideration for job responsibility and performance, both determined as objectively as possible; then, to the extent taste and greed permitted, distribute excess earnings according to stock ownership.

The consultant's report was the start of family bargaining and negotiations. It ranked the five brothers and four nonfamily managers by contribution to corporate profits, separated the rankings by percentage relationships, compared the top officers' earnings to those in industry survey reports, proposed changes in the salaries which reflected contribution, and outlined a bonus which was split between performance and stock ownership.

The salary survey showed that the president was not paid enough either in relation to CEO's of comparable companies or to compensate him for the managerial load he carried and the results he had produced. Negotiation and political sensitivity are important in family pay discussions: It is almost axiomatic that one does not cut the pay of a family member whose job has not changed. In this case no salaries were reduced; the president's base pay was increased by $10,000 to $70,000 and some minor upward adjustments were made in two other salaries. The bonus computation gave a larger share of any profits in excess of 25 percent of the opening net worth to the president, with the balance related to a combination of job performance and stockholder interest. Twenty-five percent was used because of the need to retain earnings for growth. As usual, a small amount (15 percent) was set aside for a discretionary bonus, to be distributed entirely by the two outside directors who were knowledgeable enough to make valid judgments.

In the first two years after the plan was implemented, the separation between pay and performance became clearer; the company's earnings increased so that everyone's bonus was significant. Most important, the brothers have accepted the primacy of the company's needs in setting compensation policy. The oldest brother will retire and may sell his shares back to the company; another brother may be brought out over a long term since there are too many relatives (and good nonrelatives) for him to move up as fast as he wants. Even with the number of relatives reduced, no members of the next generation want to join the company, somewhat understandably when they consider the problems their father and uncles have suffered.

CASE STUDY: HL COMPANY

Two factors made this case somewhat special: The company is a wholly owned subsidiary of a large European conglomerate whose top managers cannot be expected to stay current with American compensation practices; and the product distributed (made in Europe) was the leader in its small technical market.

There were substantial differences of opinion between the sales marketing managers and the technically trained support personnel over why the product sold: Was it the skill of the salesman who could learn enough about the product in a few months to sell it, or was the product sufficiently unique so that the selling effort was dependent on application engineering and convincing technically trained buyers of its features?

Background of Operations

Who or what creates a sale? Because a customer's original interest may develop from an advertisement, exhibition, mailer, or word of mouth, the lead time between a first contact and an order may be long. Customer budget limitations, resolution of individual technical questions, and changing purchasing personnel may cause long delays.

Inquiries are followed up by a divisional salesman in the geographic area. If he is unavailable, another salesman—different division or different area (rare)—will make the initial call and remain as customer contact throughout the sale.

The marketing manager may have a major input, particularly in specific application questions.

Performance Standards

Because the company lacks clear performance standards people do not know what they have to do to earn more, or specifically what a good job is. Every professional, that is, everyone who feels strongly about his work, sets his own standard. HL people have their own, but their subjective standards are only randomly related to the company's goals and priorities.

People would like to know how they can act differently so that their changed performance can increase their pay and help the company. "More" sales and "better" service are truisms, not definite enough to be actionable.

Develop five or six specific job standards (results) and deal with them at an annual performance review or at six-month periods. If you want to improve performance, rather than just evaluate it, separate the discussion of pay (for past performance) from what you expect in the future (job measurements) and from ways of improving performance. This can be done at one session if pay talk comes first. If there is an emotional reaction to the performance review, defer discussion about the future until the heat is dissipated.

Employees should know from regular performance review what they are supposed to do and from regular ongoing feedback where they stand. Then, future job standards and performance improvement can be discussed without being colored by the salary discussion.

Continue to review salaries after the first six months of hire, second six months, and then one year. A suggestion: Review salary and performance more frequently, at least every three months, for new hires, especially professionals.

The purpose of the review is less to adjust salary (except where original entry salary is wrong) than to give encouragement, support, and direction.

Sales Quotas and Bonuses

Establish the annual expected unit sales quota for each salesman, a negotiated figure, as the basis of a bonus program combining a quota known in advance (number of items) and reward for intangibles (hard work, problems overcome). (Comment: This suggestion was made only after interviews with the salesmen revealed that they felt it was achievable and reasonable. *Not* to find out what salespeople feel is reasonable is to create a compensation program in a vacuum. The comment is further proof that every company is unique, and the method of communicating compensation program changes must be considered with the same attention as creating the dollar format.)

Because the company's marketing policy is not just to make a sale but to make sure that the customers use HL's products well and properly, a compensation plan involving each salesman and his manager was suggested. Results come from the efforts of several people. There is little question as to which salesman eventually produced a sale. If we assume that leads are distributed fairly and that sales are proportionate to the number of demonstrations, the exposure to favoritism in lead generation becomes slim. The sales manager's influence on the sale is harder to define, but is generally accepted as significant in almost every case.

Service Department

The department's billings are divided among (1) warranty work, (2) in-house service, and (3) work on equipment no longer subject to warranty. The only true service income comes from billings to the third group, customers beyond the warranty coverage. Everything else is internal bookkeeping or part of the original selling cost.

(Comment: The question of internal billing often confuses compensation programs. Although it starts with the healthy attempt to assign accountability for divisional or functional operations, internal billing suffers from parochialism and irrelevant economics. The *company* makes money only when it deals with the outside world, selling something at a profit. A measure of performance can be established which will monitor the results of internal service—accounting, computer facilities, or equipment repair—but bonuses, which should come out of extra profits, should only be paid for performance resulting from transactions with customers.)

The departmental expenses the service manager controls should be negotiated with him. They may exclude some items now charged to the department:

□ Out-of-town repair payroll, over which he has tenuous super-
   vision.
□ Supplies made available to or used by others.
□ Warranty expense items.

Although the last items are spent by his department, they might be controlled by setting cost standards for the total expense allowed for each type of warranty repair. (Comment: Measure performance only of activities that the manager controls. Otherwise, you run into the morass of vague accountability and useless finger pointing.)

From prior history you should know the range of reasonable cost for common repairs—a scaled-down version of the TV and auto company warranty repair programs.

Quality work within expense guidelines would earn a specific bonus.

A few people might be motivated by titles, specifically McLane (to Western District Manager) and Yardley (to Director of Administration). (Comment: Use nonfinancial rewards which cost little or nothing. Proper use requires knowledge of the individual.)

Incentive Compensation Summary and Proposals

1. *Salaries and benefits:* Base salaries are reasonable and can be left alone for now. Stay in touch with area and industry figures to remain competitive. Neither a problem nor a plus, base salaries should permit the company to attract and retain the people it needs. (Comment: An independent study can confirm the appropriateness of existing salaries or provide executive assurance.)

Some of the commonly used nonfinancial benefits or cafeteria-style choice of benefits are not appropriate for HL at this time. When asked what additional incentives they would like beyond cash, no one offered any suggestions. This response is understandable in the light of the base salary levels. They are fair, but additional incentive cash payments for performance remain the most attractive inducement. (Comment: Cash is still the most popular fringe benefit.)

Cars are not proper for sales or administrative people. For the latter, there is no economic or IRS justification. The same situation exists for the sales personnel, most of whose travel is by air, not automobile. (Comment: An almost universal request of managers and salespersons who do not have a company car is to have the company pay for the individual's automobile needs. The IRS is sophisticated in interpreting its own rules on the proper business use of automobiles. Unless the company can show that its assuming the cost of an automobile is a proper and necessary *business* expense, the deduction will be disallowed upon examination. Commuting expenses from one's home to the office, the most common car use for most managers, is not a proper deduction.)

Further, the payment for the use of a car which is an obviously improper deduction creates an atmosphere of disregard for propriety which is difficult to limit. Top management's treatment of this tax regulation is probably as important in setting a tone or style as it is as a specific fringe benefit.

2. *Service manager:* An incentive plan should encourage his concern for his department's total performance. To make the introduction of a new plan successful, its results should be at least equal to the present plan for the same performance, a practical personnel procedure. Actual departmental operating figures and exact percentages can be inserted and tested against the concept.

_____percent of controllable marginal income. This is defined as sales to outsiders (the only true economic income) less related controllable expenses.

_____percent of controllable internal expenses within budget, for preparation, demonstrations, and other nonbilling activities. When budgeted expenses are more than actual and quality is maintained, a discretionary bonus of 10 percent of the savings up to 10 percent of base salary should be available.

3. *Salesmen:* Sales managers should negotiate individual unit quotas for each salesman, approved by the CEO. Because each division's sales differ, each requires a different sales quota. One

approach is to take last year's divisional sales and divide by the number of instruments sold. Unless the prior year was abnormal, use the resulting figure (adjusted for price changes) as the unit sales base.

For sales over quota, the salesman will earn 1.5 percent. For the intangibles of special effort in helping others, attendance at shows, number of demonstrations, a discretionary bonus of 10 percent of base salary should be available. Where these activities are measurable, they should be described.

Sales managers should receive .5 percent of sales over quota to credit them for their contribution and to focus their efforts on sales growth. Sales managers also participate in the corporate incentive.

4. *Corporate incentive bonus:* No incentive should be available until a reasonable return on operating assets is earned for corporate and ownership needs. This percentage should be 12 percent of the average (beginning and end of the year) operating assets, defined as all assets less cash plus 2 percent of budgeted sales for operating cash. This computation eliminates from both the income and the asset base excess cash (and its related income) maintained by the parent company for reasons other than business operations.

(Comment: The specific condition refers to the European parent's policy of maintaining large cash balances in the United States in excess of HL's operating needs. Since the rate of unearned income from investing excess cash was considerably less than that capable of being earned through operations, the cash and the related income were excluded from the performance base. If a company has *any* excess assets—land, building, machinery, investments in non-operating companies or securities—they and the related income should be excluded from performance measures.)

The incentive is based on the maintenance of the present minimum 40 percent gross margin transfer price. If the parent company reduces the margin for corporate purposes, the bonus computation should continue to be based on the 40 percent or higher gross margin. If the U.S. company is able to achieve higher margins, it should benefit. Other current intercompany charges, for example, directors' fees and intercompany salary charges, are assumed to remain at the same approximate level.

Operating income is the same as that used in the present financial statements. It excludes interest income and charges and nonrecurring subsidiary adjustments.

The 12 percent of average assets as defined should be increased one percentage point each year until it reaches 15 percent. This rate of return is commonly used by U.S. companies. When earnings are in excess of 15 percent (in any year), the excess should be split—60 percent to management and 40 percent retained by the company.

This suggestion is based on the philosophy that the investors and the managers are in partnership, in which the first, priority return is due the investors; over that base (in HL's case, set at an initial 12 percent) managers and owners share. When earnings are higher than standard (over 15 percent), management justifiably receives a disproportionate share.

It is also common practice not to limit the amount of bonus available to managers, in part for the same reasons: Only after the established ROA goals have been met do managers participate in bonuses. Thus, their payments come out of profits that might not have been earned if the incentive bonus did not exist. Since these incentive payments are conditional on profits, they cost the company little or nothing: no profits, no bonus.

To be motivating, that is, to be significant enough so that managers are likely to perform differently because of the chance of their earning a bonus, the amounts must be significant in relation to base salary. This plan offers that opportunity as shown in the following example.

Assume the average assets on which the 12 percent base is computed are $2 million. The first $240,000 of pretax operating profit is excluded from the bonus computation. Assume further that HL reports $340,000 of defined operating income. Of the excess $100,000, one-half ($50,000) is available for bonus distribution under the following formula (the percentages are the ones recommended):

President	35%	
Chief financial officer	15	
4 Sales managers		
Marketing manager	35	(proportionate
Traffic manager		to salary)
Others—in time		
Discretionary (excluding CEO so that he can be objective in its distribution	15	
Total	100%	

Salaries of the four sales managers, the marketing manager, and the traffic manager total $165,000. This group would be credited with 35 percent of the $50,000 available, or $17,500. The four sales managers and the marketing manager (present salaries about $30,000 each) would each earn a $3,200 bonus, a significant amount in relation to their base pay.

CASE STUDY: IVC COMPANY

A young entrepreneur acquired three separate businesses in different parts of the country. Each was managed by a local manager who had an individual compensation program. The questions posed were how to pay them to retain them and, if possible, direct their activities to profit making. In one case the problem was complicated by the need to interpret a written agreement which promised to give the manager stock of the local company he managed equal to the value of two years' salary.

The clearest measure of performance in the industry was cash flow—operating income plus depreciation and less debt repayments and capital equipment acquisition. More basic than the computation of the amount available for incentive bonus was the question whether pay would motivate the managers to change their performance in any way.

Investigation of the interests and goals of the managers revealed that for two of them more money was not an objective. They were fairly paid, liked their work, respected the owner's honesty, and were more interested in expanded job opportunities (which might result in more compensation) than they were in immediate increases in their salaries.

The moral of the case is simple: Financial compensation is unlikely to affect the performance of individuals who are already working close to capacity.

The amended compensation arrangements were based on cash flow in excess of 25 percent of the owner's investments and loans. In two locations the local manager received from 5 percent to 10 percent of the net cash available over the target. In the case where the manager had been promised stock equal to two years' salary, a negotiated compromise was arranged in which the manager received a small percentage of stock and for five years earned 5 percent of the cash flow that was in excess of 25 percent of the owner's investment.

Because each operation had a different history and involved different levels of management skill and talent, a single plan would have been inappropriate. Normally, consistency in compensation is an administrative advantage; it permits transfer of managers with a minimum of explanation. In this case, because the three operations were different, three compensation plans were provided.

CASE STUDY: JKL COMPANY

JKL Company is a computer software company which offered a professional-technical service, mainly computer programs, to one industry. Ninety percent of the stock is held by several large companies which founded and financed the firm; the balance was owned by six operating executives who had exercised options. The book value of the stock was currently 30 percent of the option price, and there was little hope that there would be a public stock issue for several years.

The organization consisted of a president, five department heads in charge of new products, implementation (systems analysis and programming), marketing, consultancy, and administration-finance; at the second level were 20 supervisors, group leaders, highly skilled technicians, and consultants. The balance of the staff consisted of 100 people.

The personnel were young, 97 percent college graduates with a sprinking of M.A. and Ph.D. degrees. The company had lost money heavily in its first five years, but was going to be profitable in the current year. Annual sales were $5 million.

Which new products to develop is a key decision; it is initiated by the marketing, new products, consulting, and systems executives and the president, and flows through a top committee. Development of a computer program may take 18 months.

Sales are made to many levels of prospective customers. Often a functional vice-president, controller, budget director, DP manager, and internal auditor were part of the buying decision. JKL fielded a comparable team to make the sale. Thus, it is not simple to give *an* individual credit for developing a product and even harder for making a sale.

Base salaries are competitive for the area and, where comparable, for the industry. Fringe benefits are lean; there is no retirement or bonus program.

The problem was to develop a compensation-incentive program for JKL which would satisfy the investors, attract and retain risk-taking managers, and properly reward performers.

A consultant's analysis aimed at identifying who created the profits concluded that results were dependent on the efficient functioning of groups—no one person could be clearly shown to have chosen the products to develop; no person was solely responsible for the systems analysis and programming; and, since the sale of major products ($100,000 and more) required decisions from several levels in the buying organization, no one person could be given credit for a sale.

If group effort caused the company to grow, compensation would have to be spread in the same way. Here is how the program finally evolved:

To recover their early losses the major owners insisted on an increasing rate of return on investment before any bonus was available to management. They consented to the use of book value rather than the original investment, a significant difference because of the heavy losses in the early years. Each year management had to earn 5 percent more than the starting 10 percent goal (pre- and after-tax figures were the same because of the carryover losses). The ROI goal increased annually from 10 percent to 15 percent, 20 percent, then 25 percent of the net worth at the beginning of each succeeding year. The goal rose even if the earnings in one year did not achieve that year's goal—the next higher target still had to be met.

After the ROI minimum was reached, earnings were split between the employees and the shareholders. Among employees three groups shared the incentives in proportion to their contribution to profits: the president and the five department heads received 40 percent (of which the president received one-half); the 20 managers and technicians were allocated 30 percent; and the remaining employees participated in the last 30 percent. All employees split their share of the incentive pie on the basis of salary. A 15 percent discretionary bonus was set aside in each of the three groups.

The result of the incentive program was dramatic: Put into effect in the last six months of the firm's fiscal year when the budgeted income was $200,000, the plan so stimulated activity that a $600,000 profit was realized. The bonuses for the top personnel were 70 to 100 percent of base salaries. Flushed with their success the group followed up with an even larger profit the next year. In spite of the higher ROI rate required and the higher net worth base on which it was computed (because of the first year's profit), managers still earned substantial bonuses.

With only 125 employees the company was small enough to include everyone in the incentive compensation program. Complete disclosure of financial operations, salary levels, backlog and sales data, and personnel changes was part of the company's open management style. The sharing of extraordinary profits was therefore consistent. There was also a touch of humility in the universal sharing of incentives: No one—consultant, department manager, or president—could state with assurance that anyone should be excluded from consideration because he had not contributed.

The larger bonuses earned by higher-level staff were one of the motivating influences in attracting people and retaining them. Lower-level staff sought training and accepted some dull work as a first step toward enjoying professional growth and substantial bonuses.

The discretionary 15 percent was used with care: Monthly, managers and department heads submitted the names of outstanding subordinates who might be eligible for the discretionary bonus. No superior performance was hidden. The discretionary amounts were large, and the upward filtering process ensured that the candidates chosen were qualified.

The final note on JKL was ironic: Members of the board of directors were second- and third-level managers in the large companies which had supported JKL from its shaky inception. Their salaries were approximately the same as the base salaries of JKL's young top managers. The industries attracted different people: JKL managers would not have accepted or would have left the security and institutional atmosphere of the giant corporations. After the first large bonuses were paid, members of the board moved to put a limit on the amount that could be paid to the top JKL staff.

Both the consultant who developed the compensation program and the president disagreed with the board's proposal to limit incentives. They finally prevailed by pointing out the differences in the goals, managerial turnover, and risk taking in JKL's industry compared to those of the giant corporations; and by bringing sufficient evidence that the compensation program was a key factor in the speed of the turnaround. The managers who had achieved the spectacular results and earned the large bonuses would not stay, nor were they likely to continue to work at a high level of intensity, if their compensation were not proportionate to their efforts and their results.

CASE STUDY: THE LOSS COMPANY

The Loss Company is a metal trades manufacturer. Sales total $10 million in three different plants (Table 5).

Table 5. Sales for 3 plants of Loss Company (in thousands).

	Plant A	Plant B	Plant C	Total
Annual sales	$3,000	$4,500	$2,500	$10,000
Pretax income (loss) after home office expense allocation	200	(200)	(100)	(100)

The problem facing the CEO was: What bonus, if any, should the manager of Plant A receive in the context of a corporate loss?

Small-company managers operating more than one profit center have to resolve the compensation dilemma of paying for a positive result in one operation while the overall result was a loss.

Strong arguments are used to defend the giving and the withholding of rewards. On the one hand, it could be argued that the Plant A manager made money because of his efforts, that is, he produced controllable results and should be rewarded. On the other hand, the company lost money, the Plant A manager works for the company, and to give a bonus in a loss situation is to compound a problem.

The issue touches several areas: Should the pay of all managers rise and fall on the fortunes of the total company, whose results, both profits and losses, may come from a few people or divisions? Or should managers be paid only for the results for which they personally were responsible?

The answer lies partly in the independence of the profit centers, the clarity of the decision making, and the source of profits (fortuitous, or the result of a manager's identifiable contribution), and partly in management's goal of focusing the individual manager's efforts and rewards on his operation or the total company's. If the reward system will not weaken the fabric of personal relations because it is inequitable, if it does not create a destructive win/lose situation, our preference is to reward managers whose performance justifies special consideration. The elements of a good compensation program remain consistent: Pay for controllable performance and separate levels of performance significantly.

CASE STUDY: MCS COMPANY

MCS is a chain of retail stores with annual sales of $35 million. The company is owned equally by two families, whose oldest members are first cousins. Allen is sixty-four, Harry is sixty-two; both are active but have different family situations. To provide management continuity and estate tax savings, and to retain two key nonfamily managers, the two stockholders agreed to make gifts of their nonvoting stock to inactive family members, set up a voting trust which permitted them to retain their equal voting shares as long as each was alive (deadlocks to be settled by a trusted legal adviser), and sell stock to the nonfamily managers.

Part of the plan included a retirement compensation program for the older cousin. Because the problem of what and how to pay retiring family members is common, the following excerpt from the study may be helpful:

> We suggest that Allen retire at age sixty-five and that he become a consultant in January of next year. He will be eligible for the benefits of pension and profit-sharing plans and Social Security payments.
>
> a. His consulting fee would be 70 percent of his base salary.
>
> b. His consultant's contract would include fringe benefits such as medical reimbursement, a consumer-price-index factor on the annual payments, business-use car expense, etc.
>
> c. Allen's pension and profit-sharing plans and Social Security benefits plus his consultant fee will leave him with about the same after-tax dollars as he now receives.

d. The consultant's contract would require Allen to perform his
present duties and functions, but in an advisory capacity with no
time requirements.

The IRS is concerned with reasonableness—compensation for
services actually rendered by the individual, appropriate to the
organization and the resultant performance. At the top executive
level, relationship between hours spent and value of contribution is
much less direct than at lower levels. There must be a demonstrable
relationship between the compensation and the decisions made, the
advice given, the contacts maintained or developed.

As long-term top executives move into retirement the value of
their services is related less to the number of decisions they make or
the extent of their daily supervision and more to their ability to guide
younger managers and their participation in the key decisions which
affect the company's long-range health.

Allen's involvement in the company had diminished as the two
young managers assumed increasing responsibility for daily operations. He was still important in the formation of market strategy,
acquisitions and store closings, bank relations, and the choice and
promotion of key personnel—areas that were less affected by hours
spent than by judgment and experience.

CASE STUDY: RP COMPANY

This case involves a family-owned distribution company run by a
fifty-five-year-old CEO (LR) who hired a nonfamily executive (CT) to
run one of two divisions. Total sales volume of both divisions was
$4 million. The company had been marginal before the arrival of the
new man; within a year he made his division profitable and showed
substantial potential to move it to a level it had never reached.

The goals of the compensation program: retention of the
executive as the manager of both divisions and offer to sell him a
share of the stock; an incentive bonus to the two men over a fair
return to the shareholders. Because the new executive was also in his
mid-fifties, he wanted a retirement plan. However, the company
could not afford a general retirement program. Instead, the program summarized below was proposed.

1. CT's $40,000 base salary will be retained. He will receive
annual increases equal to the percentage change in the cost-of-living

report of the Bureau of Labor Statistics. The base date should be January 1 of the current year.

2. Ten percent of the unissued corporate stock will be offered to CT at a price equal to the audited book value plus $50,000. The premium represents a modest accounting for the customer and vendor relationships.

Using the last audited year-end figures, the value of the firm is $800,000. Counsel should suggest the least troublesome way of handling the stock issuance. CT's payment can be made over three years. The offer should be available at the price and terms described for sixty days from the time of the agreement.

For the purpose of computing CT's interest in case he leaves, only the shares fully paid for (not those unpaid) will be considered his.

If he leaves the company for any reason, the company agrees to buy and CT or his estate, executors, or trustees agree to sell all his shares at a price determined by the same formula as that used in his acquisition of stock: book value as of the end of the most recent fiscal year plus $50,000. (Comment: Stock ownership is usually tied to employment.)

The company agrees to pay the amount and interest due CT or his estate over no more than five years in 20 equal quarterly payments, starting 30 days after his employment is terminated. Interest on the outstanding balance due will be at the prime rate of the bank providing the major loans to the company. If CT has worked for the company for less than three years after his first payment for stock, payments to him will be over three rather than five years. He cannot pledge the stock or use it as collateral.

3. If he leaves the company, CT shall not compete for two years within 100 miles of the company's headquarters. "Compete" shall be defined as negatively affecting the company's relations with its customers, suppliers, and employees. Proper legal language is required to make a concompeting covenant fair and enforceable. (Comment: These are common provisions of a buy/sell agreement.)

4. Participants in the management bonus shall consist of LR and CT. If others are added, their participation shall come out of LR's and CT's shares proportionately.

The bonus shall be divided 60 percent to CT and 30 percent to LR, with 10 percent distributed at LR's discretion to either of the two participants or others.

The bonus shall be based on audited pretax income. For bonus computation, LR's salary and expenses (which may be changed in the future) shall be charged to the pretax profit only at their present level, adjusted for cost-of-living changes. (Comment: This provision is a usual precaution, to protect minority or nonowning shareholders from arbitrary reductions in the bonus income.)

The bonus pool will be without limit, computed as follows:

Exclude from the bonus 10% of the combined net worth at the beginning of the year.	
On the first $50,000 of pretax income subject to the bonus,	25%
On the next $50,000,	30%
Over $100,000,	35%

Because of changing management relationships and contribution to profits, this formula and the bonus pool allocation should apply for three years.

5. Pension-retirement program for CT: Because of ERISA rules and financial limitations, a funded retirement program for CT is currently impractical. An alternate proposal is an individual deferred compensation plan.

For every full year CT has worked for the company, he will earn one year's retirement benefits. The amount due will be based on the average of CT's base salary for the highest five years (or less) of his full-time employment. The company will agree to pay CT 30 percent of the average salary for the number of years after he leaves the company (starting at age 65 at the earliest unless he is disabled) equal to the number of years that he worked. To be eligible for this deferred compensation, CT will have to work for at least three full years.

With Social Security payments, this plan provides a retirement benefit in the range of a formal plan. For example, assume CT's average base salary was $50,000 for his five highest earning years and that he worked for 12 years before his retirement at age 66. His deferred compensation plan would pay $15,000 a year for 12 years.

6. LR or his estate will give CT the right of first refusal for the purchase of the family stock at the same price and terms offered by a bona fide buyer. CT will have 30 days from notification of such an offer to match it with written notice and payment.

Finally, legal counsel will be required *after* CT and LR have come to an understanding.

CASE STUDY: TOC COMPANY

TOC is a manufacturer of heavy machinery with annual sales of $10 million and an irregular earnings history. The company's shares are owned by three active officers. The president and the treasurer each own 45 percent, the chief designer-engineer owns 10 percent. For 20 years the two principal shareholders received the same compensation. Because of varying responsibilities and contributions both men accepted the compensation equality as fair until a few years ago. As the business grew more complex the responsibilities of the CEO changed. The other major stockholder became less involved. He reduced his activities to those of a controller. The president felt that the equal pay was disproportionate to the value of the service; the treasurer felt that the present imbalance, which he and all other executives acknowledged, was temporary, and that over the history of the company the relative contributions were equal. He also deeply objected to earning less than his partner. He did not want to earn more; nor did he care if someone earned more than the two of them. He simply did not want to be paid less than his equal shareholder.

This problem—equating compensation with stock interest—is common. If the more competent person is willing to pay the price of keeping peace by giving up pay for his margin of performance, the inequality between performance and pay can be tolerated. However, we have seldom seen the superior performer not become resentful of the inequity and put pressure on the other party to accept an adjustment. When there is a power impasse, a deadlock may result which can strangle the company. (In this case the two major shareholders had an equal vote, as the 10 percent stockholder had transferred his voting rights to a trust run by the other two.)

Because TOC had such a problem, the treasurer agreed to consider a consultant's compensation proposal but not to be bound by the recommendations. The consultant urged the two principals to air their differences and acknowledge that without a settlement the company faced damage from dissension and diversion of executive energies from the needs of the business. Based on differences in the job responsibilities, salaries of $50,000, $30,000, and $47,000 were proposed for the president, treasurer, and engineer. In addition, each base salary was to be increased by a factor for return on investment. This provision overcame the treasurer's objection that although the engineer could earn more than he did, the president could not. The ROI factor (figured on a 12 percent return on net worth) brought the three base salaries to $90,000, $70,000, and $50,000. From that point two incentive levels were proposed: The first divided ROI over 12 percent on the basis of contribution (45, 20, and 35 percent), and the second was more closely related to shareholder interest (40, 40, and 20 percent).

Table 6 summarizes the computations.

Table 6. Compensation based on salary and ROI (in thousands).

	Share of Stock		
	President 45%	Treasurer 45%	Engineer 10%
Base salary (job responsibility) and 12% ROI	$90	$70	$50
First-level incentive bonus (related to profit contribution)	22	10	18
Second-level incentive (related to shareholder interest and performance)	20	20	10
Total	$123	$100	$78

Because a consultant's report has no political power, the issue was still being debated after one year. The consequences of not settling are the cooling of personal relationships and the possibility that the more competent manager will seek indirect means of satisfying the inequality.

CASE STUDY: WQ COMPANY

WQ, a manufacturer and distributor, is owned by three brothers. The older two are salesmen, while Peter, the third (50 years old), is the CEO and a major cause of the company's success. The other reason for WQ's improved operations (sales are approaching $5 million) is that Bill Monroe, a 29-year-old manager, has expanded the distibution business. Peter's concern is that Bill should not leave the company, as no one is available to take his place.

The key issue is to retain Bill Monroe by paying him fairly for his responsibility and profit contribution. The retention of Bill is not only important for current operations; it is one of the major sources of the older brothers' retirement and, eventually, of Peter's, unless the business is sold.

Within a year or two Bill should be offered the chance to buy stock; the brothers should give him some, or the corporation should consider using corporate stock as part of his compensation. It is premature to give Bill stock now. His needs are traditional for his age; he will be more satisfied with immediate cash.

A compensation program based on a formula of profit participation rather than the present discretionary arrangement should be developed. The present arrangement not only is mysterious about informing Bill what he has to do to earn more, but it probably demotivates him since it leaves entirely to Peter the decision about the worth of Bill's extra effort.

The brothers' salaries and expenses should be explained as representing, in part, a return on investment. Salaries to the family include a factor for profit distribution:

Brothers	Total Paid	Portion Representing a Return on Investment
Dan	$50,000	$20,000
Bob	$40,000	15,000
Peter	$60,000	15,000
		Total $50,000

Here is a formula for profit distribution: The company's net worth at the beginning of the year was $400,000. Before any bonus is paid, the stockholders and the company need to retain a minimum pretax level of earnings for the risk, error, and uncertainty of running the firm. Based on history and anticipated needs this is 20 percent, or $80,000. If WQ Company earned $140,000 before taxes, the amount available for bonus computation would be increased by the $50,000 paid to the stockholders through their salaries, part of which is return on investment.

The bonus computation therefore starts with $190,000. Subtracting from that amount the $80,000 set aside for the company and the stockholders, we have $110,000 on which to base a bonus. Apply an increasing bonus percentage as the company earns more:

On the first $25,000 of available profit, 10% =	$ 2,500
On the next $25,000 of available profit, 15% =	3,750
On the next $50,000 of available profit, 20% =	10,000
On any amount over $100,000	
($10,000 in the example), 25% =	2,500
Total	$18,750

If Bill is responsible for half the profits, he should get half the bonus; if Peter is responsible for the other half, he should receive that. If others are eligible because they contribute to profits (*not* because they own stock or have longevity or for any other irrelevant reason), they should participate. A limit of 50 percent of base salary would be appropriate in this case.

A Job Evaluation Program

THIS comprehensive job evaluation program was designed for a particular small company by one of the authors of this book. The program includes a discussion of how the compensation plan operates, a listing of compensation policies, a job evaluation questionnaire, a factor-point evaluation plan, and a list of specific salary classifications.

HOW THE COMPENSATION PLAN OPERATES

The method employed is a factor-point system, consisting of 19 factors chosen for their fundamentallity. The plan is designed to operate as follows:

1. Each factor has four levels of value so defined that a clear distinction is evident between each level. The levels are defined so as to avoid extensive overlapping and to make choices of the level as simple as possible.

2. Point values are established for each level of each factor. The four ratings are logarithmic in scale:

Rating	Point Value
Little or none of the factor is involved (25% or less)	1
A slight or modest amount is involved (up to 50%)	3
A sizable amount is involved (up to 75%)	6
A high degree of the factor is involved (up to 100%)	10

3. Jobs are then evaluated on the basis of the total points awarded and the job class within which the total places them. From this grouping an orderly, systematic series of grades, with point values allocated to each, is established as shown in the Factor-Point Evaluation Plan. Corresponding salary ranges are also established.

FACTOR-POINT EVALUATION PLAN

	POINT RANGES		SALARY RANGES	
GRADES	MINIMUM	MAXIMUM	MINIMUM	MAXIMUM
I			$	$
II				
III				
IV				
V				
VI				
VII				
VIII				
IX				
X				

SALARY CLASSIFICATIONS

There are 10 classes set up into which all jobs can be fitted. The classes are:

F 1   (to 20 points)
F 2   (21–26 points)
F 3   (27–33 points)
F 4   (34–41 points)
F 5   (42–50 points)
F 6   (51–60 points)
F 7   (61–70 points)
F 8   (72–83 points)
F 9   (84–96 -points)
F10 (97 and over)

4. All salaried jobs in the Company, except those of the two principals, are covered by the plan.

5. Evaluations will be performed by a three-person salary committee to be responsible for carrying out this policy and to which appeals can be made.

6. Exceptions to the committee's findings may be submitted in writing to the Secretary/Treasurer who will make the final determination.

It should be noted that it is not an objective of the plan to assure equality of compensation between jobs in the Company and comparable jobs outside the Company. We intend to pay employees as well as or better than companies with which we compete for the same personnel. What is paid for human resources will be determined by the marketplace, not by the plan.

COMPENSATION POLICIES

(a) New employees will serve a probationary period of from 1 to 3 months. At the appropriate time a performance review will be conducted and by mutual agreement permanent status will begin.

(b) Pay increases will be given only for effective performance, within the range for a job, and in the amounts indicated by the steps within the range.

(c) The spread between the lowest and highest salaries for all jobs covered by the salaried-worker compensation plan shall be 50% of the lowest salary. For example, the highest salary to be paid for a position with a starting salary of $8,000 will be $12,000.

(d) The step a person is brought in at will determine how many years it will take to reach the maximum wage for the position (for example, if a person is brought in at the third step in a range, he or she will have three annual steps remaining to the top of the range for the job).

(e) The top of the range for any position will not be exceeded under any circumstance.

(f) Raises for effective performance* will be given annually on the anniversary date of assuming the job in six steps irrespective of (and not encompassing) cost-of-living adjustments. Performance reviews may be given on a shorter period of time (for example, before completion of the probationary period). When such review results in a raise, the raise will be half of the next higher step, the remaining half to be given at the anniversary date of entering the position.

(g) When promoted to another job, the employee will serve a one-month trial period before receiving an increase. Performance review will precede any changes in salary. The increase will be to the lowest step of

---

*The review date for all salary positions will be February 1st. Raises for effective performance will be awarded based upon the Government cost-of-living adjustment for the prior year. Extraordinary performance by any employee, if documented by his immediate Supervisor and Department Manager, may be presented at any time to the executive council for special bonus-based performance award.

the salary range of the new job that is higher than his or her present salary. Future review dates will start from the date of promotion.

(h) An employee who misses two raises by reason of failure to reach satisfactory performance levels will be deemed incapable and given a less demanding job or discharged.

(i) Yearly adjustments will be made to the salary ranges to compensate for increases in the cost of living. A suitable index will be used.

JOB EVALUATION QUESTIONNAIRE

NAME_____ POSITION_____ DATE_____

All items are to be filled out. Read the questions carefully so as to be able to answer appropriately. The questions do not focus on you as a person or on the quality of your performance on the job. For example, question 1 asks what the entrance requirements for a given position are, not what the person entering the job may possess as qualifications above those required to get the job. The answer is not dependent upon your qualifications but what the job you have requires.

1. *Amount of Specific Knowledge Required to Enter Job*
   ☐ Little particular experience or education required to quality for the job.
   ☐ Some previous education and/or experience specific to the job required (examples: graduate of secretarial school, two years bookkeeping experience, combination of a year in a computer school and one year experience as a programmer).
   ☐ Qualifications for position include three or more years in a similar job or not less than two years applicable education (for example: three years or more of computer operations, two years or more of business school major).
   ☐ Qualifications include at least four years of specialized academic training or ten years of professional-level experience, or combination thereof. (Examples: accounting, engineering degrees, or 6 years as chief accountant or quality control manager. Professional certification such as CPA or PE.)

2. *Amount of Training (Cumulatively) Needed After Assuming Position*
   ☐ Job can be performed with a week or less of on-the-job training.
   ☐ Up to a month of on-the-job training required.
   ☐ Up to six months of on-the-job training required.
   ☐ Long-term training and guidance required to bring skills and knowledge to required level and maintain them there.

3. *Demands on Physical Energy*
   ☐ Energy demands are low and activities varied.
   ☐ Energy demands are modest and activities largely restricted to desk or work station.
   ☐ Energy demands are relatively high (great deal of standing or physical movement on an intermittent basis).
   ☐ Energy demands are high (constant movement or lifting or combination thereof).
4. *Degree of Concentration Demanded*
   ☐ Low level of concentration demanded (accuracy, originality, and high costs not involved).
   ☐ Some concentration required (at least one of foregoing factors involved; for example, inspector employing micrometer, checker and approver of credit, reviewer and approver for payment of invoices).
   ☐ A good deal of concentration required in work (at least one of the factors involved and some impact on costs and/or profits; for example, quality control, production planning).
   ☐ High concentration required (all three factors involved with major impact on costs and/or profits).
5. *Degree of Control Over Own Output*
   ☐ Virtually none; activities are much the same from day to day and the work load is tightly scheduled.
   ☐ Some control; activities vary slightly from day to day, period to period, on a regular basis and the work is not performed under a tight schedule.
   ☐ Fair amount of control; activities vary a good deal and are performed mainly on a time-of-completion basis.
   ☐ Large amount of control; work content is not strongly patterned (that is, demands upon position are unpredictable) and large amount of discretion is exercised in governing one's output and the priorities followed each day.
6. *Level of Supervisory Responsibilities*
   ☐ Little or no supervision exercised.
   ☐ Assigns work and directs efforts of others while performing work of the type they do (that is, supervises on a part-time basis as a lead worker or working foreman).
   ☐ Supervises primary workers (for example, production line or clerical personnel) full time.
   ☐ Supervises employees who supervise others and/or workers employing professional levels of knowledge (engineers, quality control, and production planning people).

7. *Control Over the Productivity of Others*
   ☐ Little or none.
   ☐ Some; for example, is responsible for placement of materials at work stations, producing formal schedules for performing work to be done, designing light jigs or tooling, finding improved methods for handing assigned work).
   ☐ A good deal; for example, measures productivity and takes corrective action, oversees production of work schedules.
   ☐ Great control; sets performance standards, performs value analysis, designs production layout, participates in product design from production viewpoint, initiates computer programs for sales analysis, systematically engages in methods and work simplification.

8. *Follow-through Required*
   ☐ Work usually performed in short cycles; follow-through seldom required (for example, processes mail and phone calls).
   ☐ Assignments *generally* completed within one day; follow-through seldom required.
   ☐ Work requires *some* follow-through and over periods up to one month.
   ☐ The bulk of work performed involves follow-through over long periods of time.

9. *General Volume of Decision Making*
   ☐ Makes no original decisions (all decisions made under policies and/or close direction).
   ☐ Occasionally makes original decisions (10% or less).
   ☐ Makes as many original decisions as decisions under policies or direction.
   ☐ Makes mostly original decisions.

10. *General Level of Decision Making*
   ☐ Decisions have little effect upon cost or profits.
   ☐ Occasionally makes decisions with low impact on cost or profits.
   ☐ Often makes decisions with low impact on costs or profits.
   ☐ Makes many decisions which have appreciable effects on costs or profits.

11. *Span of Intra-Company Contacts Entailed*
   ☐ Contact primarily limited to same department.
   ☐ Has occasional contacts on routine matters with one other department.
   ☐ Has contacts on routine matters with several departments.
   ☐ Has widespread contacts on matters usually affecting costs or profits (for example, coordination of operations, implementation and progression of projects).

12. *Customer Contacts Entailed*
     ☐ No customer contact (other than internal phone and paper flow required).
     ☐ Some customer contact at routine level (for example: shipping clerk).
     ☐ Heavy customer contact at a generally routine level (for example: order processing, credit, collection).
     ☐ Heavy customer contact at the highest level of significance (for example: selling, sales promotion, market research, product testing).

13. *Outside Contacts with Other Than Customers*
     ☐ Little or none.
     ☐ Some, at a generally routine level (for example, vendor expediting, trucklines, contractors).
     ☐ Heavy, at the operational level (for example, purchasing).
     ☐ Heavy, with some impact on fulfillment of corporate plans (for example, R&D, legal, advertising, sales promotion).

14. *Ability to Affect Sales Volume*
     ☐ Little or no influence.
     ☐ Some ability to affect sales volume (for example: delivery scheduling).
     ☐ Can affect sales volume indirectly and over the long range (for example: through quality control and purchasing).
     ☐ Work bears heavily on sales volume (for example: marketing planning, sales management, product development).

15. *Ability to Affect Profits/Profitability*
     ☐ Little or none (work highly routinized and controlled).
     ☐ Work bears indirectly on profits (for example: inventory management).
     ☐ Some of work bears directly on profitability (for example: production management).
     ☐ Work primarily oriented to production of profits (for example: marketing, R&D).

16. *Authority to Spend Company Money*
     ☐ Does not spend company money.
     ☐ Spends money within budget *only* (as previously authorized).
     ☐ Spends money within established guidelines (for example, as authorized by purchasing policies, blanket purchase orders).
     ☐ Spends money outside budget, subject to approval.

17. *Quality of Written Communications Involved*
     ☐ Little or no written communications originated.
     ☐ Communications mostly limited to entering data on forms, in records or books.

☐ Originates summary documents, regularly issued reports.

☐ Does considerable original writing (for example: originates proposals, business directives, and/or guidance documents).

18. *Contribution to Sense of Direction*

☐ Does not contribute to setting of objectives, plans, policies, or budgets, at any level.

☐ Contributes to such within the department only.

☐ Originates objectives, plans, policies, and budgets at department level.

☐ Participates in the formation of the firm's overall corporate plans (that is, has an active voice in forming corporate objectives, plans, policies, and budgets).

19. *Influence upon the Development of Others*

☐ Has little or no influence on the development of others.

☐ Trains and counsels employees with similar skills and pay within a department.

☐ Trains, counsels, and plans the development of supervisors, middle-level managers, and/or professionals within a department.

☐ Trains, counsels, and plans the development of department heads and professionals (such as engineers, product development specialists, accountants).

A Compensation
Survey

THIS survey, which has actually been used frequently by the authors, has proved to be a good way of determining the attitudes of managers—not only on matters of compensation, but also about their relationship to the firm and to the employees whom they supervise, the general atmosphere at work, and their own personal aspirations.

1. How do you feel when you tell people what firm you work for?
   (1) Proud __ (2) Good __ (3) Just a place to work __
2. Do you think the firm offers you the chance to have the kind of job that you will want five years from now?
   (1) Yes __ (2) No __ (3) Not sure __
3. To what extent are you made to feel that you are really a part of the firm?
   (1) Not at all __ (2) To a small degree __ (3) To a large degree __ (4) In every possible way __
4. Do you feel that favoritism (in making assignments, giving raises and promotions) is shown in the firm?
   (1) None __ (2) Very little __ (3) Some __ (4) Much __
5. To what extent do you understand just what work you are supposed to do and what your duties are?
   (1) Very poor understanding __ (2) Fairly good understanding __ (3) Clear understanding __
6. Do your supervisors on the job set a good example in their own work habits?
   (1) All of them do __ (2) Most of them do __ (3) Some of them do __ (4) None of them do __

7. When you want information or help on a difficult problem, how likely
    are you to get the help you need? I get:
    (1) Very little help __ (2) Fairly good help __ (3) All the help I need __
8. When changes are made in the work you have done, how often are you
    told the reason for the change?
    (1) Rarely __ (2) Sometimes __ (3) Usually __ (4) Always __
9. When you are corrected or when your work is being criticized, how
    often is this done in a way helpful to you?
    (1) Sometimes __ (2) Usually __ (3) Always __
10. Do you find the work assigned to you challenging and interesting?
    (1) Sometimes __ (2) Usually __ (3) Always __
11. Are you encouraged to offer ideas and suggestions for new or better
    ways of doing things?
    (1) All the time __ (2) Often __ (3) Sometimes __ (4) Rarely __ (5) Not at
    all __
12. What progress have you made with the firm?
    (1) Excellent __ (2) Satisfactory __ (3) Some __ (4) Little __ (5) None __
13. In general, how well do you like your present position?
    (1) I like it very much __ (2) I am satisfied with it __ (2) I neither like nor
    dislike it __ (4) I dislike it __
14. How do you believe you are paid relative to your worth to the
    company?
    (1) Very fairly __ (2) Adequately __ (3) Unfairly __
15. How do you believe you are compensated relative to others in the
    company?
    (1) Very fairly __ (2) Adequately __ (3) Unfairly __
16. In general, how do you feel about the workload expected of you?
    (1) I should like to have more work to do __
    (2) The amount of work expected is reasonable __
    (3) The amount of work expected is somewhat too great __
    (4) The amount of work expected is unreasonable __
17. How do you rate the polices on vacation, holidays, and other payments
    for time not worked?
    (1) Excellent __ (2) Good __ (3) Fair __ (4) Poor __
18. How do you rate the polices on group medical insurance, life insurance,
    and similar benefits?
    (1) Excellent __ (2) Good __ (3) Fair __ (4) Poor __
19. What attention will your personal problems be given if you bring them
    to the firm's attention?
    (1) Substantial attention __ (2) Some attention __ (3) Not much atten-
    tion __
20. What opportunity for advancement do you have in the firm?
    (1) Much opportunity __ (2) Some opportunity __ (3) Little opportu-
    nity __ (4) No opportunity __

21. When you were interviewed for employment, were the opportunities described fairly and honestly?
    (1) Not as good as described __
    (2) Fairly and honestly described __
    (3) Somewhat better than described __
    (4) Much better than described __
22. When you started to work for the firm, how were the training and help you received?
    (1) More than I needed __ (2) All I needed __ (3) Almost all I needed __
    (4) Less than I needed __ (5) Very little __
23. Does the firm keep you informed about its activities and plans?
    (1) Always __ (2) Usually __ (3) Sometimes __ (4) Seldom __ (5) Never __
24. As far as you can see, are the main decisions of the company generally made on the basis of the needs of the firm or according to private judgment and interest?
    (1) According to the needs of the firm __
    (2) According to private judgment and interest __
25. In your opinion, is management of the firm primarily client/customer-oriented or does it primarily serve the interests of the owners?
    (1) Primarily client/customer-oriented __
    (2) Primarily serves owners' interests __
26. As far as you can see, are employees treated as being basically intelligent, capable, and willing, or as unreliable and not intelligent?
    (1) Intelligent and capable __
    (2) No consistent treatment __
    (3) Unreliable and not intelligent __
27. Is your performance measured against some standard you know in advance, or on the basis of someone's opinion?
    (1) Performance judged against standards __
    (2) Performance judged on basis of opinion __
28. Are employees promoted or given pay increases because of what they contribute to the company, or because of other reasons?
    (1) According to contribution __
    (2) Other reasons __
29. Is management willing to share the contributions to profit made by employees?
    (1) Yes __ (2) No __
30. On a scale where 10 is the highest use of your abilities and skills, what number represents the way the company is using *your* capabilities and skills? __
31. How do most employees feel about the firm?
    (1) They are loyal and conscientious __
    (2) They are indifferent __
    (3) They really don't care __

32.   Is the management atmosphere in the company open, with sharing of
      views, information, and power—or is it secret and closed, with informa-
      tion withheld?
      (1) An open, frank atmosphere __
      (2) A closed, withholding atmosphere __
33.   Considering the opportunities which were available to you, do you now
      feel that you chose the right job?
      (1) I prefer this job to any other __
      (2) I like this job better than most others __
      (3) I sometimes wish I had chosen some other job __
      (4) I definitely wish I had chosen some other job __
34.   If you were able to start again, do you feel you would go to work with
      our firm?
      (1) Yes __ (2) No __ (3) Don't know __
35.   What do you think of this opinion poll?
      (1) I like it __ (2) Probably all right __ (3) I don't like it __
36.   What can be done to improve the performance and/or working
      conditions in the company? Mark those of the following needing
      considerable improvement:
      (1) More clearly defined goals __
      (2) Better internal communications __
      (3) Better company planning __
      (4) More frequent staff meetings __
      (5) Improved understanding of each person's responsibilities __
      (6) Improved physical surroundings __
      (7) More sensitivity to customer/client needs __
      (8) Sound, fair performance standards __
      (9) More qualified people __
      (10) Better employee indoctrination and training __
      (11) Improved staff productivity __
      (12) More or better equipment __
      (13) More regular and factual salary review __
      (14) Broader participation in decision making __
      (15) More room for development and advancement __
      (16) Other_____

Please answer the following:
      __ Male   __ Female
      Number of years with company: (1) Less than 1 year __
                                      (2) 1 to 3 years   __
                                      (3) 4 to 6 years   __
                                      (4) Over 7 years   __
      Department _____

Index